VINCENZO
VENEZIA

healing for daughters
of emotionally
absent fathers

Ways to Cope with the Emotional Aftermath of Having
an Unavailable and Rejecting Father, Including
Processing Grief, Anger and Childhood Wounds

ISBN: 979-12-81498-11-2

TABLE OF CONTENTS

INTRODUCTION

A child has a lot of needs that must be met in order for her to feel safe, loved, and protected from harm. A child's needs begin when she is a baby and continues throughout her childhood and adulthood. Just as a child requires food, shelter, clothing, and medical care, an emotionally secure relationship with both parents is essential for healthy emotional development. If a child is unable to meet the essential emotional needs of a mother or father, and if she cannot find those needs in the other parent, she will be at risk of developing emotional problems. Although a child has two parents in her life to work as a team in meeting her needs, the bond between a father and daughter is especially strong.

It is often noted that the relationship between a father and his daughter is unique and often stronger than the relationship between a mother and daughter. A father can give his daughter unconditional love, which helps her to develop self-esteem. She knows how loved she is by her father regardless of her appearance, personality, or accomplishments. He models for his daughter how to love others and value them on their own merits rather than their appearance or popularity. Although a mother can give her daughter unconditional love, it is often expressed in a different manner than the love shown by a father. A father shows his daughter how to be loving in ways that a mother does not always show.

When he fails to provide such guidance and support, it can cause her to develop emotional problems as she grows from childhood into adulthood. Depending on the nature of the emotional abandonment and the quality of the father's role in her life, a daughter is at risk of developing emotional problems. Emotional abandonment influences a daughter's ability to develop a healthy relationship with others afterward in adulthood.

When you were young, you often did not understand why your fathers were in the situations they were in. You assumed it to be normal for him as a man. You may have thought he must've been working hard and loved you whether or not he told you so frequently. Because of this, it seemed very natural for men to go through periods of emotional absence throughout their lives. However, as you matured and gained more life experience, your adult self's needs changed. It is much more difficult for an adult to understand why their father is emotionally absent than it was when they were a child. One of the biggest questions that each missing father figure leaves in their children's lives is: "Why do you not love me?" Each time you are disappointed, you question that love that connects you to your father.

There are many reasons why fathers are emotionally absent in your life, and it is important to understand them. This is not meant to blame the father for your emotional problems but to understand why he could not or did not fulfill your needs and expectations. This will allow you to heal many of the emotional scars you have from your childhood. Understanding why he left you is important to answer the question: "Did I do something wrong?" You may feel a sense of guilt or shame because of his absence in your life. This takes place when you develop an identity that associates your value with his presence or absence.

This book aims to open your eyes to the many issues affecting women with emotionally absent fathers and the relationship you have with them. It will help you determine where your pain stems from, which will allow you to address each issue that sets off the memories related to why he is emotionally absent in your life. You will also learn strategies to work through the pain you experience and how to build self-esteem and confidence, which is essential for emotional stability and recovery from emotional wounds.

PART 1
- IDENTIFYING
THE SYMPTOMS
OF EMOTIONAL
ABANDONMENT

CHAPTER 1: DADDY ISSUES AND ATTACHMENT THEORY

The formation of emotional bonds between a mother or father and a child begins at birth. Early interactions with them will serve as the model for all adult relationships later. This includes romantic relationships that you will have throughout your lifetime. A mother and father's role significantly impacts a child's social development, academic performance, and overall adjustment. They also differ in the ways they interact with their children.

During childhood, some individuals have distant or nonexistent relationships with their fathers. Others may be too close for the relationship to be healthy. Both scenarios can contribute to the development of "daddy issues." Although commonly used, "daddy issues" are not an official mental health diagnosis. Some individuals relate to the term "daddy issues." Others believe it minimizes their emotional experience and trauma by placing blame on the individual who endured it rather than recognizing its complex origins.

Even women in stable relationships may be told they have daddy issues if their dating patterns or sexual orientation do not conform to cultural norms regarding sexual attitudes and behaviors.

Daddy Issues and Attachment Theory

A difficult relationship with a dad can negatively impact anyone, not just women. Freud and the Oedipus complex may have introduced the concept of daddy issues. According to the theory, a child forms a strong attachment with a parent of the opposite sex and harbors feelings of competition toward a parent of the same sex. Freud observed this behavior in both boys and their mothers.

For instance, when a boy develops an attachment with his mother, he feels hostile toward his father because they compete for the love and affection of the same caregiver. These unconscious feelings of hostility and rivalry toward the opposite-sex parent may be represented in a variety of ways.

Soon after, the complementary theory was developed by Carl Jung, a student of Freud, and focused on similar emotions that female children may experience. The female version is named the Electra complex. It is named after a legendary character from an ancient Greek tragedy, Electra, the daughter of King Agamemnon and Clytemnestra.

Although most psychologists no longer adhere to these theories, they help explain how cultural beliefs about daddy issues may have developed.

John Bowlby's attachment theory, which is a more recent psychological explanation, says that your earliest relationships with the people who cared for you shape how you connect with people as an adult. Childhood experiences with a mother or father that were positive will create an adequate model for future relationships. On the other hand, relationships that are traumatic are remembered and contribute to developing daddy issues.

When an individual's primary caregiver is emotionally unavailable, unable to set limits for the child, or lacks empathy for the child's needs, the caregiver does not adequately meet the child's needs. Such distressed relationships leave a lasting emotional imprint on the child that may be expressed in a variety of ways.

Types of Needs

A daughter has two primary needs that her father must work to fulfill. It is the physical and psychological needs; if either of these needs is not met, emotional problems can develop.

1. Physical Needs

The mother can meet a daughter's physical needs, but since she is the primary nurturer, this need may be more suited for someone else. The father is more likely to fulfill this role because he is perceived as being more objective and independent of the child. The father can provide physical security to the daughter. The ability to give her the confidence that she can be physically taken care of is an important aspect of her emotional development.

He should provide the following physical and emotional needs for a daughter:

a. Protection

The physical needs of a daughter are met by her father when he provides the fulfillment of physical protection against other outside forces that may threaten her, like real dangers or emotional dangers. He needs to protect her from physical harm as well as emotional harm. He gives her the feeling that she is safe when he is present with her.

There are two ways that he can protect her physically:

I. Directly Protect her From Outside Forces

It is important that the father protects his daughter from out side forces that are actually a threat to her well-being. He can protect her by monitoring her surroundings and providing her with realistic safety and security. She will feel safe when she is with him because he will be able to provide physical protection to keep her safe from real dangers, like outside parents who may take advantage of her or a school bully, for example.

By doing this, a father ensures his daughter that she is safe while she is with him. This also provides her with a feeling of trust while he is with her. This will help her have the ability to feel secure physically, which means that she will not have to feel like she is always on guard and have the feeling that danger can come from anywhere at any time.

II. Provide Her With Realistic Safety and Security

The father can also provide his daughter with realistic safety and security by providing her with a sense of well-being. This may be done by giving her confidence in her ability to have control in certain situations.

The father who takes time to show his daughter that she has control over certain activities allows her to feel safe and secure because she has the knowledge that she can take care of herself. This helps her feel safe and secure while he is with her because she will not have the fear of feeling powerless. This is especially true when her father provides opportunities for her to take risks and have fun because playing with different people can be exciting and completely safe while engaging in various activities. By participating in sports or doing other activities that are fun, she will learn how to control her feelings and put them into action without becoming overwhelmed or scared by them.

The father's protection for his daughter is meant to prevent her from feeling lonely, scared, or unsure about anything. With this as a foundation, she will have the knowledge and confidence to deal with everything in her life without fear of the unknown, which is the natural outcome of being human.

b. Proximity

The physical needs of a daughter are met by her father when he provides the physical closeness she alone desires. She will not feel lonely or afraid when she is with him because she will know that someone will always be there for her, provide support, and nurture her in any critical situation.

There are two ways that he can provide her with proximity:

I. Physical Movement

The father provides physical movement by moving around and physically interacting with his daughter frequently while he is with her. He should be seen as a mobile force that is ever present in his daughter's life and not just someone confined to one location for extended periods. This allows her to feel like she can always approach her father and that he is not a closed-off entity that is only available at certain times. This allows her to feel that she can approach him with any problem, and he can provide an answer for her or give some form of support.

By being seen as constantly in motion, the father is able to demonstrate how his presence alone gives off an impression of safety and security. This is done by demonstrating how he is actively involved in his family's lives by being present with them, which causes them to feel safe because they know there will not be any unknown dangers around them as long as their father is nearby. The physical closeness gives her a sense of empowerment because she feels part of something bigger and more important than herself. By experiencing this feeling, the daughter can learn how to express her power in various activities, such as playing sports or taking leadership roles in various activities at school, because she is willing to be a part of something bigger than herself.

II. Physical Connection:

The physical connection that a father provides his daughter with is through physical touch. This is done through a process of non-verbal communication and visual cues that allow her to feel safe and secure when she is with him.

Non-Verbal Communication:

The father demonstrates physical connection by demonstrating physical contact with his daughter. He needs to provide her with signals of affection through touching, hugging, kissing, caressing, and holding hands while they are together. He can give these non-verbal messages in many forms, such as holding hands or standing close to her while they are together, which the daughter will interpret differently at different ages. The most important thing that he needs to do is demonstrate obvious affection toward his daughter. This will reassure her that she is safe and protected and that he loves her.

Visual Cues:

The father can also demonstrate physical closeness through visual cues because it is a form of nonverbal communication. He will be able to show his daughter what he thinks by how he looks at her and treats her. He will do this by looking into her eyes, touching her arm, or holding hands with her while they are together. The most important thing that he needs to do is demonstrate that he is looking at her and not just seeing through her. When this occurs, his daughter will feel connected with him because she knows that he recognizes her as an individual. This will give her the feeling that he respects her, which will give her a sense of respect for herself. These feelings work together to establish a strong foundation for trust and safety between the two of them, which will last throughout their lives.

The father is seen as a mobile force who is always present in her life through his actions of physical closeness and touch, which shows her how he feels. This demonstrates how he will be there for her while giving off an impression of security by being in constant motion with her. This allows her to feel safe because she knows that there are many people around to support and help her at any given time, which empowers her because she knows that she can do whatever she wants.

c. Organization

A daughter meets her physical needs when she feels organized and safe within the environment that her father provides for her. This could mean that he creates a structured environment that is welcoming to her, his wife or partner, and any other children they may have together. This environment should not only provide her with a certain level of security through protection but also welcome her into it by creating a structured yet simple and functional environment for her. This will allow her to know that she can rely on it for comfort, encouraging her to explore and discover new things about the environment and how she can use it to fit the needs she has.

There are two ways that he can provide his daughter with the organization:

I. Organization in the Environment

The father can provide his daughter with "organization" by locating various resources and items that will allow her to feel safe, including him providing her with food, shelter, and clothing.

The father's ability to provide these items will allow her to have a sense of order and safety because she will know that he's taking care of while being able to have the opportunity to explore other aspects of her environment. This will also allow her to know that he is looking out for her and protecting her as he helps organize these resources in an orderly fashion so that she can access them whenever she wants.

II. Organization in the Family

The father can meet his daughter's organizational needs by providing her with a structured family life. This allows her to feel safe and secure by knowing that there are certain expectations she will follow, as well as having the opportunity to explore and discover what is going on in the environment of the family. This will also allow her to feel organized because she is able to rely on the stability of her family by knowing the roles that everyone plays in their daily activities. She will know what is required of her and what she can expect from others, which allows her to feel safe by knowing that she can trust the environment in which she is living.

The father who provides his daughter with an organized environment and family life allows her to feel safe and secure by her knowing that she is able to rely on the stability of her home environment. He is responsible for ensuring security in their home by providing basic necessities like food, shelter, and clothing. This will allow her to feel valued and respected because he has taken care of her needs so that she can learn and explore what it means to follow through with her responsibilities in meeting the family's expectations. This provides a strong foundation of trust and safety between them, which extends throughout their lives and can be used to recognize her contributions to the family.

These physical needs of a daughter, which make her emotionally stable and secure, are crucial for her development. As a child grows and becomes more aware of the world, it is important to understand that most physical needs can be filled in other ways. This is mostly because children learn how to show what they feel with their bodies as they get older. Physical needs can be fulfilled if the child is given opportunities to develop other skills and talents that will later allow them to meet their needs more effectively.

2. Psychological Emotional Needs

The mother and father can meet a daughter's psychological needs, but the father is more likely to be needed here because he is perceived as more objective and independent. The psychological needs of a daughter are for her to develop a sense of emotional balance in life, which allows her to develop strength in her mind.

The father should provide the following psychological needs for his daughter:

a. Independence

The father should encourage his daughter to develop independence by allowing her to have a sense of self-reliance and confidence in her environment. This will allow her to explore the world and discover that she is able to take control of her life and live it on her own terms without feeling dependent on another person or environment. This can benefit her by allowing her to include herself in activities and gain a sense of self-confidence because she has the tasks that are important for survival and growth.

There are three ways that a father can provide his daughter with independence:

I. Physical Independence

Whether the father is providing for all of his daughter's physical needs or working alongside the mother, he should allow her to feel independent by having her to take care of herself. This will give her a chance to discover how she can rely on herself and develop a sense of self-awareness by understanding how she will complete each task necessary to keep the home organized. This will also give her the opportunity to develop a sense of competence and efficiency by doing it on her own.

This will also give her the opportunity to grow in confidence because she will be able to explore and discover new aspects of herself that she was not aware of previously. By being independent, she will develop a sense of empowerment in knowing that she is able to set her own goals in life and achieve them through hard work.

II. Emotional Independence

The father should allow his daughter to feel emotionally independent so that she can grow up while recognizing her emotions as a way of finding comfort and expressing herself. This is an important part of emotional well-being because it allows her to feel secure and stable in life by being able to know how she feels and why she feels that way. This will allow her to express herself by talking about concerns or problems as well as develop a sense of empathy in knowing that she can take on someone else's perspective without feeling threatened or offended because she recognizes her emotions and knows how to manage them.

By having independence in her emotions, she will be secure in how she feels and recognize how others are feeling. This allows her to develop trust and respect for the people around her because she is able to connect with them through sharing similar experiences and feelings. This will also allow her to have a deeper connection between herself and her siblings because they can discuss their feelings about the family or other concerns they may have.

III. Social Independence

The father should also allow his daughter to feel socially independent so she is able to learn how society works on an interpersonal level. This will allow her to form social relationships with other people and understand how they feel in the same situation. This is an important part of life because it enables her to form bonds with others while also maintaining her individuality and independence in relation to them. She will have the opportunity to explore different ways of relating with other people so she can learn when she needs to stand up for herself as well as accept help from others.

This will provide a sense of stability for her later in life because she will be able to establish meaningful, healthy relationships without feeling dependent on them all the time. Her social independence will also help her develop social skills such as conflict resolution, negotiations, and decision-making. These skills will help her in the future because she will be able to negotiate effectively with others, make decisions without feeling threatened, and resolve conflicts without losing control of herself.

Independence is an important psychological need for a daughter because it develops her independence and self-reliance. This will allow her to explore the world around her, become more confident in herself, and decide whether others can relate to her on an equal level.

b. Sense of Identity:

The father should provide his daughter with the opportunity to explore who she is and how she wants to express herself so she develops a sense of identity. This is important because it enables her to understand how much individuality she has, which gives her a chance to make decisions based on what she feels is most important and valuable.

There are three ways that a father can help a daughter form a healthy sense of identity:

I. Exploration:

The father should allow his daughter to explore who she is and give her some room to try out different theories about what type of person she wants to become. This will allow her to develop self-awareness and self-confidence because she will discover how she feels about certain aspects of life and why. By having the freedom to explore what is important to her, she can find how her values compare to those around her and decide what her priorities are in life by figuring out what matters most to her.

By exploring who she is and what type of person she wants to become, she will have the confidence and motivation to work toward those goals and achieve them because she knows what she wants and how to achieve them. She will be able to feel a sense of hope that is not false or imagined because it has been built on the foundation of truth and reality, so she will continue to be motivated when times get tough.

II. Flexibility:

The father should be flexible in how he deals with his daughter because that will allow her to feel confident in directing her own life, even if there are times when she cannot do so. They can do this by being open to changes that come with age and keeping a flexible attitude in allowing her to make decisions as she grows.

This will also allow her to develop good habits because they are not based strictly on following a plan. This will allow her to become comfortable making different decisions because she can make them in a natural way. This will also give her room to grow up at her own pace and make mistakes in certain areas because there are no consequences for letting things go wrong. She can learn from her mistakes to develop a sense of responsibility for the mistakes she makes.

If she feels that the father is flexible, she will be more flexible with herself and others because there will not be a lot of pressure placed on her to accept one specific idea about who she is supposed to become. This will allow her to express herself freely and not give up on ideas that she likes, even if others don't like them. She will also better understand how to deal with different people by allowing her to experience life from many different perspectives.

III. Encouragement:

The father should encourage his daughter to live her own life authentically regardless of what others say about her. He should do this by encouraging her to find what makes her happy and pursue it at all costs. This is important because it will provide her with a sense of motivation by giving her the support she needs to follow through with the decisions she makes.

If the father is supportive of his daughter in this way, she will have the security to express herself naturally and not be afraid to admit if something does not work for her. This will allow her to find out what does and does not work for her without feeling ashamed or being made fun of by others because they can accept that everyone makes mistakes.

The father can also do this by encouraging his daughter to become independent from him and others, enabling her to pursue a sense of fulfillment on an individual level rather than becoming dependent on others for happiness. She will learn that happiness comes from finding what she loves and pursuing it at all costs because she has mastered herself and her motivations, so she does not need to rely on other people for a sense of fulfillment.

The father's support and acceptance of his daughter will enable her to develop a healthy sense of identity by providing her with opportunities to explore and find out who she really is and encouraging her to live authentically regardless of what others say about her. This will allow her to feel personal satisfaction, able to express herself without feeling pressured by others. She will also feel motivated to follow through with the decisions she has made because she knows that they are right for her since they have come from where she comes from.

Physical needs alone do not make a girl healthy; they are important in providing physical nourishment and protection. However, emotional needs are critically important in her development as a functioning individual who will thrive in adulthood and in all areas of life. The type of support she receives from a father figure during her early years has profound effects on her ability to mature as an adult and develop healthy relationships with others throughout life.

CHAPTER 2: THE EFFECTS OF EMOTIONAL ABANDONMENT OF A FATHER ON THE ADULT DAUGHTER

U nfortunately, not every daughter is able to experience a good relationship with her father, which is usually the result of some form of emotional abandonment. According to a 2022 report by the American Psychological Association, studies indicate that as many as 43% of all girls experience some form of emotional abandonment while they are growing up. While it is normal for a girl to experience some level of frustration with her father at times, it is not normal for a father to completely shut down his emotional connection with his daughter, and the possibility of being emotionally abandoned by your father should not be taken lightly.

Signs and Symptoms of Emotional Abandonment

Every girl should know the physical and psychological symptoms of emotional abandonment.

You may experience these symptoms at some point in your life if you are not receiving the necessary support from your father figure. They include:

Physical Symptoms

1. Inability to Focus and Pay Attention

A girl who was emotionally abandoned will also have difficulty staying focused on tasks at a consistent level. This is because you will naturally become bored whenever there is not much action in your life. You get easily distracted because you need more motivation, which means you cannot focus on one task or activity for a long time without becoming bored and distracted.

To further explain...

Your attention will always drift elsewhere, whether it be checking your phone for messages, scrolling through social media, etc. You may also find yourself growing bored with whatever you are doing after only a few minutes of doing it. You will need help balancing your priorities and keeping yourself focused on one task throughout the day.

When asked why you are so easily distracted, you may find yourself needing help to give a proper answer. You may be chasing a dream which you chase so hard that it eludes you, or it could be that your feelings are repressed, and everything is expressed as physical symptoms of emotional abandonment. You are constantly giving your brain and body a "numbing" sensation by being distracted and repressing emotions, which is why you cannot focus on just one thing and concentrate for a long time.

2. Sudden Drop in Your Energy Levels

An emotionally abandoned girl will also be more easily worn out than other girls her age. This is because she will experience an "out of energy" feeling before she goes to bed every night. Your body will be drained of energy, and your mind will only see one or two things that it wants to focus on. This makes you face the prospect of going to bed early and not being able to sleep well because nothing is "interesting" enough for your mind to want to stay awake.

To further explain...

The sudden loss of energy is because your brain is depleted of all of its serotonin, dopamine, and norepinephrine. All of these neurotransmitters are responsible for energizing your body and giving you cognitive alertness, concentration, and motivation throughout the day. It is all caused by the traumatic experiences you faced in your earlier years of life and the lack of attention you received from a father figure. When these neurotransmitters run out of your system, you will suddenly become fatigued and unable to think clearly.

You will also have sudden drops in your energy levels throughout the day. You may feel like sleeping all day long or binge eating to compensate for the lack of energy that you have inside. You may lose physical activity without knowing why, or you may not even be able to sleep through the night without waking up for one reason or another. You are constantly competing against low levels of neurotransmitters, which is why you may be unable to stay awake for very long during the day, or all of your energy will just run out overnight.

3. Loneliness

The most common symptom of emotional abandonment is a feeling of loneliness, which is a result of the repressed and unresolved emotions that are still within your body and mind. You will feel a perception of loneliness when you are alone, in a room, or with other people.

To further explain...

When your repressed emotions have not been dealt with properly, they will all begin to surface. As a result, you will have a range of feelings that are unique and specific only to you, which will cause a type of loneliness inside of you that can be overwhelming at times due to the fact that no one can ever really understand what you are going through. It makes you realize how alone you are despite having multiple friends online or on social media. You can never feel that it is enough to fill the void of loneliness that will always be within your heart, mind, and soul.

This is a result of the father figure not being able to properly deal with your emotions in the past, which is why you are unable to get that validation in your life and feel good about yourself when you are around other people or just by yourself. You may even feel that everyone is against you and that you live in a world of fear and distrust. The loneliness inside you is like a tumor that will continue to grow every day until you learn to release the emotions trapped inside you properly.

4. Enjoys and Creates "Drama."

You are an avid movie and television viewer, which has led you to believe that drama is an essential aspect of life. You think that you can use this to escape from reality. It is easier to watch the consequences of other people's actions rather than deal with your own problems. This causes you to develop an emotional attachment to the problems in other people's lives.

To further explain...

You can see how other people deal with their problems and get back at others for their actions or words. You enjoy watching movies about war, fighting, or revenge because it makes sense and lets you understand what people go through to deal with real-life problems. This makes you create your own drama-filled stories and use them as an escape from your own reality.

You cannot recognize how other people react to situations they are put into. You cannot see the personal impact that someone's actions or words have on others.

You enjoy creating your own drama stories and using them as an escape from reality, which causes you to constantly be focused on the negativity in other people's lives rather than what is happening in yours. This will cause some people to avoid being around you because you make yourself seem like a victim of other people's actions or words when really, it is never really about you.

5. Aggressive and/or Self-Destructive Behavior

Abandonment by your father figure can cause self-destructive behavior and aggression, which is why you tend to have anger and rage inside of you. You feel trapped in a dark hole from which you cannot escape, and you do not know who you are without your father figure's love and approval.

To further explain...

You have no idea how to channel those emotions in a positive way and will always resort to violent behavior whenever you feel like your back is against the wall. You become defensive and aggressive around people, which is why they label you as someone who cannot get a grip on reality. You feel as though you are going crazy because you have so much bottled up within your soul and body that needs to be released for your own benefit.

You become overwhelmed and emotional because of the smallest things and will react accordingly. You have a bad temper fueled by the abandonment you suffered at the hands of your father figure, who was supposed to be there to help you deal with life on a daily basis. You do not know how to express yourself properly without getting upset, so you will resort to violence to get your point across.

6. Substance Abuse

Substance abuse can further compound the problems that you have when dealing with emotional abandonment, which is why you use things such as drugs or alcohol to hide your feelings. You also use these substances to escape reality for a little while for you to pretend as though nothing has happened. It is a form of self-medication that you use to make yourself feel as though you are in control of your actions.

To further explain...

You were never taught how to deal with the emotions you were experiencing properly, so you turned to substances to express yourself. You use substances to numb yourself from the harsh reality of life and want to forget about it for a little while. The substance that you choose may not always be the one you thought it was going to be, which is why you will have to experiment for you to find out what works for you.

The abuse of drugs and alcohol can cause you to be a lost cause, which will cause you to continue down the same destructive path that you have been on for years. It will cause you to lose yourself completely and no longer be able to function as a productive member of society. It will cause you to become violent, aggressive, and emotionally unstable.

7. Social Isolation

You have a pessimistic outlook on life and believe that there will always be individuals who mistreat you. This causes you to avoid social interaction, making it hard for others to see how much this affects your daily life. You never learned how to deal with others, which is why you are always afraid of what to say or do to them.

To further explain...

Since you were never taught how to socialize and interact with others properly, you will isolate yourself and refuse to see anyone on a personal level. You believe that everyone else is out to get you, and the only time you will let them see your true emotions is if they are going through something worse than what you have experienced in life. This negative outlook on life causes other people to avoid being around someone who has suffered emotional abandonment. You are not able to see the positive aspects of life, and you do not see how other people truly react to you.

8. Anxiety & Panic Attacks

You have anxiety and believe that life is always going to be perfect no matter what. You are unable to deal with minor problems that arise in your life because you believe that everything will turn out well. You cannot comprehend when things do not go according to plan, which causes you extreme anxiety when it is time to solve a problem.

To further explain...

You do not understand personal setbacks, and you have a hard time believing that everything will work out in your favor. You are always in panic mode because you have never experienced personal failure, which has caused you to panic and not know what to say or do.

You believe that life is perfect and that nothing will ever go wrong, which causes you to get frustrated at minor issues that occur in your daily life. You are not able to think about the future or how this will affect your daily actions toward a problem, which causes a lot of stress when it does come time for you to take action in a situation.

When it comes time to take action because of a problem, you will go into panic mode and have difficulty understanding why things are not going according to plan. Your fear of failure can cause you to deny the severity of a situation, and you will constantly think that everything will work out in your favor. If this continues, it can cause you to become very sick in your mind.

9. Obsession with Misunderstanding

You have an innate ability to spot hurt feelings and become extremely sensitive to criticism. You fear being ridiculed, which is caused by the emotional abandonment you received at the hands of your father figure. You begin to wonder why you are always criticized for situations that you do not create but rather come from another person's actions or words. You constantly look for ways to get back at other people for things they say or do, which will cause intense resentment in their hearts.

To further explain...

You are unable to see the impact that your actions and words have on other people. You believe you always have to do your best and that others do not care about the consequences of their actions toward you. You believe that others take pleasure in hurting you, which is why it is difficult for them to see how badly this causes you to suffer.

You seek revenge on others for their actions towards you, which will only hurt them in return. You cannot see why this hurts them so much and causes further consequences in your life. You are not able to see the impact that your actions and words have on other people. You find yourself becoming obsessed with understanding the emotions of others. You can only understand the feelings of people you always criticize, which is why you always comment on them and constantly try to get under their skin.

These physical symptoms are merely a catalyst that will incite the mind, which is why you will have to deal with them for you to see the truth of your situation. The symptoms occur to help you see the truth of your emotions as they were shown to you during your childhood. It is important that you find out why these symptoms are occurring and what happened to stop them.

Psychological Symptoms

1. Low Self-Esteem

This is a symptom that can always be present in people who have suffered from emotional abandonment during their childhood. You believe that you are not worth anything and are not wanted by the world. Your self-esteem is so low, and you feel you will never be able to attain anything that matters to you. You were never taught how to love, respect, and care for yourself. Since no one has ever shown you what it is like to be hugged, loved, and told that everything would be okay, you will experience a lot of doubt regarding your self-worth.

To further explain...

You do not know who you are and will question everything about yourself on a daily basis. Since you do not know who you are, you believe the worst things about yourself to be true. You don't think much of yourself, which makes you shy, quiet, and self-conscious around other people. You develop insecurities about your appearance and find everything you do wrong. Since others judge you harshly for how you look, dress, talk, etc., it becomes difficult for them to see your good qualities. This creates more doubt in your mind and will cause more issues with self-esteem.

Your father figure is part of the reason you have low self-esteem and do not feel good about yourself. Since he was never there to show you how to be a loving person, you have no idea how to deal with your emotions properly as they occur. You were never taught how to express yourself around others when it comes to what is going on in your life.

2. Creeping Doubt

You find yourself always doubting the actions of others and how they will impact your life. You cannot trust anyone because you always assume that they will hurt you in some way. You never feel safe around others, which causes a lot of anxiety when you are forced to be around other people. You feel as though everything is up in the air, and you cannot trust anyone to guide you through difficult situations.

To further explain...

You find it difficult to believe what other people tell you and think about doing, which causes tense relationships with most of your friends. You question the advice people give you and have difficulty putting your full faith in other people's hands. It is difficult to put your trust in someone else when you do not know if they will hurt you in the end. When people make promises to you, you begin to wonder if they are trustworthy and if they will uphold their end of the bargain.

People who have suffered from emotional abandonment during childhood experience a lot of doubt and nervousness when it comes to trusting others. You always think that everything bad that happens to you is your fault and that everyone is always against you. You have a hard time believing that others care about your feelings, which makes it harder for them to care about what is going on in your life.

3. Depression

You begin to feel as though something is wrong with you for no reason at all. You have no idea why you feel this way and why you are not in a better mood. You try to ignore these feelings, which are merely a form of a temporary escape from reality, and continue with the day as though nothing is bothering you. You do not realize that this is an emotional response to the abandonment that you have suffered at the hands of your father figure.

To further explain...

You become disconnected from reality and experience a lot of anxiety because you are unsure how to deal with your feelings. You internalize everything you are going through, making it difficult for others to see how badly you are suffering from emotional abandonment. You begin to question everything about yourself because of these feelings and believe that there must be something wrong with you for feeling this way.

You start to feel like you are a burden to the people in your life and that they would be better off without you. You begin to wonder why you are unable to be happy, open up, and enjoy the pleasures of life. These thoughts become very consuming and will affect every aspect of your life. You become the type of person that is always depressed about something or for no reason at all, which will cause others to distance themselves from you to avoid any more pain that you are causing them.

4. Fear of Failure

You are afraid of failure, which is caused by the emotional abandonment you suffered at the hands of your father figure. You were not taught how to work hard and make anything you put your mind to happen. You never learned how to deal with failure, nor could you handle it when it occurred. Since your father figure was never there to help you when things went wrong, you always blamed yourself and felt as though you did everything wrong.

To further explain...

You were never shown how to deal with failure, which will cause you to give up on everything you do. You have no confidence in yourself and will rely on the opinions of others for every choice you make. Your life is filled with personal failures, which have led you to question yourself on a daily basis. You have a hard time dealing with what has happened and who you are as a person. You constantly look at others to see how they have dealt with their own personal issues, which causes you to become discouraged. You think that no matter what you do, you will fail and never reach your goal.

You were not taught how to deal with failure, and it will cause you to become very hard on yourself when things do not go according to plan. You constantly doubt yourself since you have no idea how to deal with anything that has happened in your life properly. You believe that the world is against you and that it is impossible for things to ever change for the better. Your father figure was never there to help you overcome your insecurities, which caused you tremendous amounts of pain and suffering. You cannot see that you are not a failure, but an individual that can overcome anything they put their mind towards. Your confidence in yourself is at an all-time low, and you will never feel like you can accomplish anything independently.

5. Overly Needy for Attention And Validation

You feel like no one in your life is good enough for you. You look to others for validation and constantly need someone to believe in you. You want someone to tell you that everything is going to be alright, but you do not have the confidence to tell yourself that. Since your father figure abandoned you, there was always a voice in the back of your head telling you that you were not good enough and never accomplished anything on your own.

To further explain...

You constantly look to others to tell you everything will be alright. You want people around you so you can have someone to talk to when things go wrong. You try to please everyone in your life but often feel as though you need more. You can never feel that things are improving and believe no one loves or cares about you. You feel judged by everybody and like an outsider looking in on everything that is happening around you. You don't want to be alone, but you don't want anyone to talk to you or judge you.

You are constantly over-worried and afraid that you will continuously fail at everything you accomplish in your life. You think everyone is against you and have no idea how to reach out for help when things go wrong. Your father figure abandoned you when they were supposed to help, which caused you to grow up with a lot of insecurities about what it means to be a man. You feel as though you do not have much in common with everyone else, which is why you need so much validation and attention. This is the only way you know how to deal with your feelings because you never learned how to be honest with yourself or the people around you.

6. Inability to Trust Others

You have no idea how to trust the people in your life because the ones who are supposed to be there for you are not. Since your father figure abandoned you when they were supposed to protect and guide you, you look at everyone else as though they will do the same thing. This causes you to become very distrustful and afraid of trusting anyone for anything at all. You will question everything they say and do because you are afraid that they will abandon you when things get difficult.

To further explain...

You never learned how to trust others because your father figures never taught you how. You always believed that everyone was out to get you and would question everything they said to you. You did not want to be mocked and ridiculed, so you became the type of person who would not say a word about anything out of fear. You have a complete lack of faith in others, causing you to take everything they say with a grain of salt. You feel as though you cannot trust anyone and are afraid of being taken advantage of by everyone you meet. You are so paranoid and cautious that you will not take any chances with the people around you. You believe that everyone is out to hurt you, which makes you push people away for fear of them hurting you even more.

You have no backbone and are constantly afraid of standing up for yourself. You allow others to walk all over you and think so little of yourself that you will allow people to treat you the way they want. You would rather take the abuse and be in pain than deal with what life has thrown at you. You feel that your father figure was never there to protect you, which is why you fear trusting anyone else with your heart. You need more confidence and are a desperate character that no one can get through to. You never learned how to deal with things yourself, which became apparent when you were younger and felt abandoned by the people who were supposed to care for you.

7. High-Focus on the Past and Dwelling on the Negative

You spend all of your time dwelling on the events of your past and the individuals who have wronged you. You constantly dwell on the past and can never move forward from it. Since you feel that your father figure emotionally abandoned you, you constantly think about all of the horrible things that have happened in your life. You are always reminded of how they never cared about you and left you to deal with everything alone. No matter how many people try to help, you do not want them in your life because they remind you of everything that has happened.

To further explain...

You have no idea how to deal with your negative emotions because no one was ever there to support or guide you through anything. Even if people are trying to help, they will still need to find a way to do so. You care too much about what happens in the future and let others drag you down into a pit of negativity where nothing good will ever come from it. You are so caught up in the past that you could not care less about what is happening now. You want to think about everything that has happened to you, which causes you to forget about the things that are going on around you.

You have a hard time moving forward from the past, which causes you to think constantly about everything you have been through. You never let the good things in your life get to you because you are too busy dwelling on the horrible things that have happened. You consistently think about all of the pain and suffering that has happened throughout your life. No matter how many people are there for you, it does not make a difference because anything anyone does will not change the way you feel about them. You feel like you were put on this earth to suffer, so you constantly wallow in your own misery and pain.

8. Fear Authority Figures

You tend to fear authority figures such as police officers, teachers, coaches, or anyone in a position of power that you may have to deal with in the future. When you were a child, your father figure was the person who you looked up to and admired. When your father figure emotionally abandoned you, you were left to deal with all of the negative emotions and feelings that came from this. You never learned how to trust authority figures, or anyone for that matter, and do not know where you stand with anyone.

To further explain...

You feel like you had no father figure in your life, so you never learned how to respect or look up to authority figures. Since they were never there to guide you or teach you how to be a good person, you are scared of anyone who has this type of power over others. You never feel safe around authority figures because you are afraid they will put you in a situation where you will feel abandoned again. You fear the fact that they can hurt you and easily break your trust because your father figure did it so easily when he emotionally abandoned you.

You are so scared of authority figures because you do not know where you stand with them. You are afraid that they will put you in a situation where you will be hurt and left alone once again. This causes you to look at them as your enemy instead of someone who is there to guide you in life. You are always questioning their actions because you want to make sure that they will not hurt or abandon you again. It is hard for anyone to gain your trust when they do not know where they stand with anyone.

9. Lack of Faith and Desire to Be Forgiven by Others

You have no faith in anyone and no desire to be forgiven by others. This causes you to have a hard time believing that others ever have your best interest in mind. You believe that everyone is out to get you and that people only care about you when they need something from you. You never experienced forgiveness in your life, which is why you have a hard time feeling remorse for your actions.

To further explain...

You have no desire to be forgiven because you have never been given the opportunity to be forgiven. Because you have not been shown that there are consequences for your actions, you are a very angry person who does not care what others think of you. You will constantly begin to criticize other people, which does nothing but cause you more stress and earn you hatred from others.

You will never understand how others can forgive your actions because you were never shown that this was possible in your life. You believe that no one ever forgives anyone, which causes you not even to try to show remorse for your actions. You are always blaming others for the way you feel because you were never shown that people could change or forgive you for any of your actions. You have never heard that being forgiven by others is possible and would not know what to do if someone said it was possible.

You have no idea who you are as a person or who others are as people. You have never figured it out because of all the different things that have happened to you throughout your life. The only thing that has remained constant throughout the years is that others could never care less about what you think or feel about yourself or them.

To further explain...

You can never figure out who you are because you have never been told who you really are. Instead of learning who you are, you were always told that something was wrong with you and that you needed to be fixed. You have been taught that what others think of your actions is the only thing that matters, not what you think about them. You are so confused about who others are because nothing in your life gives it substance and meaning.

You do not know who you are because nothing is consistent in your life. You might have known who you were in the past, but now there is nothing around to remind you of your identity or who you really are. Everything in your life seems overwhelming because everything constantly changes, leaving no one place to escape or be safe. You have no idea who others are because there have been times when they pretended to be someone they were not just to get what they needed from you. You have no idea who you are because you have never been shown who you are or how you feel.

The physical and psychological symptoms are all very similar because the same issues cause them. If you suffer from one form of these symptoms, then it is likely that you will experience the other as well. The physical symptoms can impact your psychological health in a multitude of ways. Not everyone will be able to recognize that they are suffering from one or all of these symptoms, but it is important that they do. If you were to suffer from emotional abandonment for an extended period, then psychological symptoms would almost be guaranteed. It is very hard for someone to live with constant pain and not find relief in some coping mechanism.

CHAPTER 3: HOW EMOTIONAL ABANDONMENT CAN AFFECT ROMANTIC RELATIONSHIP

A happy and successful relationship is the result of both parties working together to meet the needs of each other. Both parties must be willing to put their partner's needs first and show them selfless love. There is no doubt that a romantic relationship is not always easy, but it is more than worth putting effort into. A relationship can also be very rewarding when both parties respect one another and are willing to work together to make each other happy. When one or both parties do not care about their partner's feelings or put in any effort, it can cause an emotional rollercoaster ride for both partners.

A father emotionally abandoning you as a child will negatively impact how you relate to men in your life, particularly the men you are romantically involved with.

The following are the various ways how you can possibly behave in a romantic relationship with a man:

1. Constantly Testing His Love

You do not believe your partner will ever really love you, so you continuously test them in every way possible. You do not believe that they can be serious about you because everything they do is simply a test to determine how far they can push your buttons before you react.

To further explain...

You constantly test your partner's love because you have been shown that no one ever loves or cares about you and that this will always be the case. You have learned from past negative experiences that no one will ever love or care for you, which causes you to constantly test them to find out just how far away from "real love" they really are.

You constantly test your partner because you do not know who they really are deep down inside. You do not trust them because you do not believe in true love. You believe that they are only testing to see how much abuse, pain, and suffering they can put you through before you decide to end the relationship for good. You are afraid that if you truly love them, they will hurt you in a way you cannot explain or understand. You believe that they love you because they want something from you, which is the only reason you should allow them to love you in the first place.

When your partner can no longer figure out why you keep testing him, he becomes confused and thinks something is wrong with you. This will make him feel hurt, frustrated, and upset because he never knows what you want from him or why you constantly try to prove to him that he does not love or care about you. This confusion makes it impossible for your partner to progress with his feelings towards you because he always wonders if the next thing he does will be why the test starts all over again. Your partner may eventually give up on his feelings because he believes they are not returned or will never be returned by you.

Once your partner no longer believes in true love and gives up on his feelings, it eliminates the possibility of a successful relationship or marriage. You will have wasted all the time, effort, and energy your partner invested in you by constantly testing his feelings. This will cause both parties to be emotionally hurt and exhausted without resolving their conflict. You will have wasted years of your partner's life on something meant to be just a test, so nothing ever changed.

2. Excessively Jealousy

You often get jealous if your partner spends time with someone else, even just a few minutes. You do not believe you will ever be enough to satisfy your partner's needs, so you always assume he wants someone else to fulfill those needs. When your partner can only spend a short amount of time with you, it really hurts and makes you feel very envious because you want him to spend more time with you.

To further explain...

You are so used to feeling invisible and unimportant that it is easy for you always to assume your partner wants someone else more than they want you. Because you feel this way, you cannot allow him to spend time with anyone else. You are afraid that if he is spending more time with someone else, it means that he loves them more than you and that they are your replacement. You are afraid that they will come and get it from you if you give up your spot. You have often felt replaceable in the past and do not want to feel that way again, so you cannot allow others to take your spot. You are afraid that even if you give up your spot, you will still be replaced by someone else because this is how much your partner truly wants the other person.

To make matters worse, you are always afraid that you will be replaced by someone else who is better than you. This fear causes you to feel insecure and jealous when your partner is spending time with anyone else because deep down inside, you believe there is always a better choice out there, and they will always choose them instead of you. You do not believe that someone would ever want to be with or love someone like yourself, which causes negative thoughts and feelings towards your partner.

Jealousy will be present in any relationship because other people always want your partner, but it becomes a problem when it is consistent. It becomes a problem when it takes over your entire relationship, and you can no longer be happy or enjoy being with your partner. When you are always jealous, it is not difficult to see why any type of progress would be impossible and that your relationship will never work out in the long run. Your jealousy causes you to be fearful and paranoid, which makes it impossible to stay in love and enjoy spending time with your partner.

Your partner will eventually get tired of feeling like they can never do anything or be with anyone without worrying about what you will think. They will begin to feel suffocated and controlled by your jealousy, making them feel like you are abusive and possessive towards them. They will not know what to do or say because they are being accused of doing something that they did not even do in the first place.

You may think that jealousy will eventually stop, but it will only worsen as time passes. Your partner will eventually become so used to your jealousy that they start to believe it is normal, and they will begin to feel suffocated by the constant suspicion that you always have of them. This will eventually cause them to give up on their feelings for you because they do not believe that you can ever get over your jealous nature.

3. Doesn't Know How to Work Through Relationship Problems

Whenever you are in a relationship, you can either work it out or leave it. You cannot solve your problems if you do not work through them, but sadly, you do not know how to work through any issue or problem that may arise in your relationship. You either pout, cry, rant, walk away, clam up, or do anything else you can think of to avoid the problem and the issues in your relationship.

To further explain...

You have never been able to work through issues, struggles, or problems in your past. Being emotionally abandoned by your father figure in your childhood has caused you to feel too scared or insecure ever to have the opportunity to work through anything. You do not know how to work through any problem, struggle, or issue because you have been told to let it all go and not worry about it. Because of this, you have never been able to think for yourself, so you are afraid of anything outside of what you have been taught to do.

Being taught never to deal with anything and let it all go has caused you to believe that everything outside your comfort zone is a threat and a problem that must be avoided at all costs. You have learned that solving problems is for other people and that it is a sign of weakness. This has caused you not to desire to solve issues or work through problems because you do not believe that you can ever be successful at anything. This is why your relationship issues have continued for as long as they have, and you will never be able to progress.

Your partner will eventually become frustrated because they want to work through issues, but you always avoid them at all costs. They will become so used to your avoidance that they eventually stop trying to work through things and give up. They will believe it cannot be worked through because you have never been able to do so and become too scared or insecure about the subject. They will feel like there is no point in trying because they will never be able to work through anything, which leads them to feel like you will never solve their issues. This will cause many problems in your relationship because you will never be able to move forward and make progress.

This is why you need to make some changes because this type of problem will continue to cause issues in your relationship. It may or may not seem significant at the moment, but it is, and you have much to make up for. You can never continue to avoid problems and issues because this will only cause your relationship to fall apart around you. The longer you continue this behavior, the worse it will get and detract from your relationships.

4. Chooses Emotionally Distant or Unavailable Men

You always have a choice of who you want to be with. Deep down inside, you know what is best for yourself, but for some reason, you always choose men who are emotionally unavailable or distant. This is not something you do consciously; you will never see why or how you do it, making it harder to change.

To further explain...

You have a specific type of man you are attracted to and a certain personality you like in men. You will always gravitate towards men who are emotionally unavailable and even domineering because you have an emotional void in your life that needs to be filled. Also, they remind you of your father figure and childhood, and you subconsciously think they will care for you the way your father figure never did.

You believe that this type of man is what you deserve because of your past and how you were emotionally abandoned in the past. Your father figure was not there for you when you were a child, so now, as an adult, you are looking for a man to take care of you, take away all your problems and worries, and hold you when you are feeling insecure or sad. In your mind, this is the only way to find true love and happiness because you were not given that chance as a child.

They bring up memories of your childhood and how you felt desperately in need when you were being abandoned, which is why you always choose distant men because it feels familiar. This is the only way your mind can explain why the men you choose always fill this void and make you feel secure. This is not because it is meant to be, and you will never see the real reasons why you do this, but it does not matter because this is how your mind and heart work. Your past has caused you to confuse love and protection with abandonment, but it is not your fault, and you cannot change it, but you have a choice on whom you want to be with.

You must learn more about yourself and realize you deserve more in a relationship. You are not stupid, you are not less than others, and you do not need to settle for anyone who cannot love and respect you how you want to be loved and respected. You can avoid this type of man in the future and choose someone who will care for you and treat you with the love and value you deserve.

5. Expects a Man to Create Happiness

You expect your partner to provide you with happiness be-lieving they have the power to create happiness and a sense of security in your life and do not believe that you can do so by yourself. You feel like your happiness depends upon them; if they are gone, so is your happiness.

To further explain...

You have been trying to find happiness in every relationship because you believe it is impossible without a man. You expect them to provide you with happiness for being in a relationship with them or just being themselves. Because of this, you can never be happy or find happiness on your own, so you rely on someone else to give it to you. This causes you to depend on them for your happiness and completely ignore that they need their own happiness.

You also cannot find your own happiness because you cannot make yourself happy or be satisfied with life. You will always feel like something is missing from your life because it is not the same as if they were there with you, which makes it hard to be content. This causes you to think that you are entitled to some happiness or that someone should ensure you are happy. This will cause you to be unhappy always and feel like your life is meaningless without a man or someone who can offer you solace.

The idea that they could make you happy is the biggest reason why relationships never work out in the long run, especially if you both have this problem. You do not believe that anyone can ever love you and be in a relationship with you for who you are but instead for what they can gain from it. You take advantage of your partner's feelings for you and abuse them when things get difficult. You believe that since they love you, they are responsible for ensuring you are always happy. You are unwilling to do anything to make them happy outside of the relationship because you believe they must do all the work. You believe that they should be the ones to make sure that you are productive in your life so you can feel happy and confident.

This will make your partner feel like they have to work even harder to make you happy because they are the one who is responsible for making you happy. It will make them feel emotionally used and manipulated by you, making it impossible for you to ever create a meaningful relationship. They will eventually become fed up with your feelings and demand that you start caring for yourself instead of them, which will ultimately cause them to end the relationship, even if they are still in love with you.

6. Overly Flirtatious

Even if you are not in a relationship or do not have a man in your life, you tend to go out of your way to ensure that a man notices you. You may even flirt with others just for the fun of it. You love the attention you receive from other men and how nice it makes you feel when they look at you.

To further explain...

You constantly believe that you are not good enough, and you need to be told constantly that you are attractive by others to make yourself feel worthy. You will even ask your partner if they still find you attractive or if they like how you look when other men are around because it makes you feel good about yourself. You must always be reassured that you are still attractive, or you will start questioning yourself.

Because of this, you will always be flirtatious with other men. Other men make you feel special or wanted, and you think they appreciate you for who you are. Whenever a man is interested in you, you will flirt back and give them the impression that you want to be desired by them. You will not be able to stop yourself from noticing how good it feels to be desired and that other men are interested in you, which causes you to flirt.

The issue with this is that you are making it a point to flirt with every man that comes your way, which makes you a lot of work. Your partner will eventually become tired of this, and over time, they will realize that you are always looking for someone new just so you can be desired for who you are. They will stop believing in your attraction towards them and see you as someone who is flirty. The jealousy from this can cause them to subconsciously think it is because they do not make enough of an impression on you or are less attractive than other men. This causes your partner to believe the same about themself and feel insecure about their love for you, which, in the long run, causes you to be unhappy and unappreciated.

7. Uses Sex to Affirm Your Self-Worth

You feel like their love is the only thing you need to feel secure and worthy of respect, so you trade sex as a form of validation to make sure they accept you. You believe that sex is the way to get them to love you and give you what you need; without it, you do not think they will care about you as much.

To further explain...

You feel the only way to get your partner to love you is through sex because this is how they show affection for you. You see it as a sign of their love and respect for you and want them to continue with these signs of affection. You have been using sex as a form of validation to show them that you are worthy of their love and affection, so it is difficult for you to be with a man who does not want sex.

Even if it means giving your partner what they want sexually and not something else, you'll do anything to keep them interested in you as a lover, which is why you are always willing to do anything for them. You try to do everything that they want sexually and will go out of your way if it means avoiding rejection by them. You will even give them more sex than they want because you believe this is the only way to prove your love for each other and ensure they keep loving and respecting you.

This will make you feel ashamed of yourself and like you are less than other women, which makes it difficult for you to be with a man who does not have the same ideas about sex. Without sex, you do not feel like you have anything to offer your partner, which causes you to feel worthless and like you have nothing to bring to the relationship. This is because you have been trying to use sex to make them care about you, as if you are a prize they can win by having sex with you. You are willing to give them all of the sex they want to win their affection and love for you, which is what causes this problem in the first place.

If you use sex as a form of self-validation, your partner won't respect you or feel they can trust you. They will feel like they have to earn your affection by doing things you should be doing for them instead of expecting reciprocity. They will also feel obligated to give you sex instead of affection, which makes it difficult to be with you. You cannot create a meaningful relationship if you always rely on sex and sexual acts to make your partner stay with you.

Most men will also not want to be with a woman who only cares about sex, even if they do feel the same as you do. They will believe that you are only using them for sex, which makes it difficult to have a healthy relationship. You will be unable to form a meaningful connection with your partner because they know they cannot rely on you as a lover and cannot trust you. Men want women who care about and love them, not those who only use them for sexual pleasure and affection.

8. Makes Many Negative Assumptions About Men as a Group

You believe that men are inherently bad and incapable of ever truly loving someone. You believe they all want to use you for sex or to make themselves feel better about their lives. Because of this belief, even if they aren't using you, you will always be on guard when involved with a man. You constantly look for signs that they will hurt you somehow and are preemptively angry with every man because they might do so.

To further explain...

Even if you have a partner who is nothing like this and treats you with complete respect and love, you will not trust their intentions because of this belief. You will always be skeptical of their feelings and intentions toward you and constantly question their love for you. You will not trust that they are telling the truth when they say how much they care about you because you will believe they are lying and want something from you.

You believe that all men are like your father figure, who did nothing but neglect you emotionally and physically. You believe a man does not know how to love someone and cannot love anyone unless it benefits them. This is why you completely ignore the fact that the man could love you because you are just waiting for him to leave or hurt you at some point. You believe being with a man who truly loves and respects you is impossible, so you avoid serious relationships altogether and stay single.

This will make it difficult for a man to be in your life because you will view all his actions as suspicious. If he tries to hug or kiss you, there must be something else behind it other than pure affection, even if there isn't anything sinister about it. You will always think he is up to something, even if there isn't. If he says you look good, it must be a trick to seduce you or mean he is just trying to make you feel better about yourself somehow. Your mind will always be on alert and looking for things that may not be true to avoid harm because you believe men are untrustworthy and evil. This can make it very difficult for the two of you to build the type of connection and relationship necessary for happiness, creating a toxic environment for both of you instead of a healthy one.

Every man is different and should not be generalized as a whole. No one can ever prove that all men want sex or will hurt others to get it because you cannot prove their intentions. Some men have bad intentions but still become good people and make the right choices for everyone involved, just like some women do. You will never be able to see this or believe that a good man can exist or have good intentions because of your beliefs about all men. You will always see the darker side of a man and never assume anything about them other than the worst scenarios possible.

9. Date Much Older or More Dominant Men

You will always date older or more dominant men because you believe they are more mature and can handle being with you. You choose them because you feel like they are more able to be with you and treat you the way that you need. Your past has caused you to look at this type of man like they are your savior and the one who will fix all your problems. You will go out into the world seeking the type of love you didn't get from your father figure as a child.

To further explain...

You were never given the love and value you needed from your father figure, so now you are looking for a man to give it to you. Deep down, this is what you believe that love is and how it should work. You know that your father figure did not love you the way you needed, and you are looking for this type of man to make up for how he did not improve your life.

You believe that this type of man is the one who will truly be able to love and take care of you. You will choose older or more dominant men because they seem more mature and hold adult responsibilities. You will think that this means your relationship with them will be more stable and that they will understand your needs and give you what you need. You may believe that this type of man is what you need to make your life better and safer.

However, this does not always happen; sometimes, your relationship will be harsh for no reason. You will blame him for how things are because he is older or more dominant than you and will think he has too much control over you, but it is not true. You created this problem yourself by not speaking up or getting help when you needed it before, so now it is his fault because he made his feelings clear when they were never clear before.

You must change this behavior because you will always end up with the wrong men. You will never be able to settle down and fall in love with a man who deserves you. You will always be looking for someone more mature or dominant than you, but this is not what love looks like, and it is not a good sign for your future relationship. You need to learn how to keep yourself safe so that you can move on and find stability in your life without having no one to take care of you, without feeling empty inside when you are with your partner, and without making the same mistakes over and over again, because it does not get easier with time.

10. Patterns of Abuse

Growing up with a father figure who was emotionally absent and abusive has caused you to associate these things with love, so you now think it is normal for anyone to be abusive. You believe that this behavior is how all relationships work and that it is acceptable for someone to be emotionally abusive. It does not matter who the person is or their age; you will always think it is okay for someone to be abusive towards a person.

To further explain...

You have been raised under the impression that all people are evil, manipulative, pretentious self-centered individuals. You have learned that people are only out for themselves, and it does not matter what anyone does or says because they will always be mean and manipulative. You believe that these things are normal, so you cannot see anything wrong with being an abuser or being abused by someone. You perceive abuse as normal, meaning you will never be able to see the warning signs of it or be aware that it is happening to you.

You think emotional abuse is acceptable because it did not cause you much harm as a child. You have only recently grown up, but your father's effects still live inside your head and your personality because you are still learning to deal with and process your emotions. You have never been taught to deal with and process your emotions effectively, so it is easy to fall into your old habits of mistreating others and allowing them to treat you like trash. You believe that when being treated like this, you deserve it for not doing anything about it, which has caused you to feel bitter and resentful towards anyone who has ever treated you differently than you deserve.

You have never been shown how to break your patterns of abuse and have learned to accept abuse as normal for a relationship. Your partner will eventually become frustrated with you because you will continue to be abusive towards them. They will feel like they can never get through to you or change you because of what they believe is an uncontrollable behavior on your part. You see nothing wrong with how you treat people because it is the only way you know how, but this behavior will create problems in your relationship and cause it to fall apart around you.

As your father figure has emotionally abandoned you, this will affect your relationships. Your past has that much of an effect on your actions, emotions, and behavior, so you need to break out of this cycle, heal, and move on. You do not have to keep living your life in fear, hurting others, and being hurt by others over and over again when you can face this head-on and get help.

PART 2 - UNDERSTANDING THE EMOTIONAL ABSENCE OF THE FATHER

CHAPTER 4: COMMON TYPES OF ABSENT FATHERS

No father is perfect, but absent fathers are far from perfect fathers. Emotionally absent fathers come in many different shapes and sizes. How a father raises his child will differ from how another father raises his. It is not about how they are different but how they all share the same trait of not providing the right type of parenting that makes it easier to categorize them all into one group–emotionally absent fathers.

The difference in how they act, what type of parenting they provide, and what kind of emotions they show separates them from each other. Each type will differ in how they contribute to their daughter feeling emotionally abandoned.

The following are the common type of absent fathers:

1. Physically Absent Fathers

They are there, but they are not really there. They typically work up to 12 hours a day and only spend a few minutes with their children, and some work out of town or have moved to another region. These fathers are also working to provide for the family, but their work keeps them away from their children. This type of absence is very frequent nowadays, especially with the busy lives that most of us live. In fact, caring for the family is a secondary purpose to most people. The primary reason that they are working is to provide for their family and still maintain a decent lifestyle.

It does not mean that physically absent fathers do not love their children as much as fathers who are around; it just means that these fathers may not know how to show their feelings, and the only way they can do this is by providing for their children's needs. Because of this, children will be left confused as to why they never see their fathers. Many will worry that their fathers do not love them as much as other kids. To counteract this, these children will grow up feeling a sense of abandonment and, consequently, anxiety, anger, and depression.

- *"Why doesn't my dad love me?"*

- *"I wonder if dad will ever come back home?"*

Those are typical questions children may ask when their fathers are physically absent. For example, in 2022, the number of men working in the USA increased to 72.4%, according to National Center for Health Statistics. These people are also known in America as the breadwinners. They are typically more generous, but this does not mean they are better fathers–just different. They may be emotionally absent but are still there to care for their families.

2. Abusive Fathers

These fathers are not so much emotionally absent as they are violent. They express their emotions in a very destructive way. They use their physical presence to frighten their children and cause them emotional distress. These abusive fathers are not necessarily absent, but they have different kinds of relationships with their children than emotionally present fathers. They interact negatively with their children, so they can be considered emotionally absent because they do not provide a safe and comforting environment for their children to feel loved and protected.

Physical abuse is not the only type of abuse that physically absent fathers can commit. Both physically present and absent fathers can commit emotional and sexual abuse. Emotional abuse includes cursing, ridiculing, criticizing, or name-calling towards the daughter without regarding how it affects her mental state.

It also includes ignoring or rejecting a child for an extended period for no reason due to anger or rejection towards that child because she does not adhere to his ideals or the ideals of a certain group he belongs to. Sexual abuse includes all forms of sexual contact between an adult and a minor, regardless of whether it is consensual or not; this will be explained further below.

In the article "A study of psychological and sexual abuse in the lives of US children," it was found that approximately 2.1 million children are abused each year. The most common type of child abuse is physical, estimated to be one-third of all reported instances. It was also found that more than one in five neglect cases involves a male caregiver (parent) and a female victim. It also found that an estimated 270,000 children are abused each year, involving more than one in five cases of sexual abuse. Physical abuse and sexual abuse are the most common types of child abuse, but male parents and older siblings more commonly commit emotional abuse. Emotional child abuse was also found to be most common with younger children ages 1 to 3. Furthermore, it is estimated that girls are at a greater risk for exposure to sexual abuse. This is because children tend to be more open with their fathers, thus enabling them to commit this crime.

No matter what type of abuse it is, all these children will experience a great amount of emotional trauma and confusion. Having an abusive father is a great emotional burden for a young girl, especially since she is too young to understand the meaning of what is going on.

3. Critical Fathers

A critical father does not accept and love his daughter's thoughts, ideas, and decisions. He may actually make his daughter question her own thoughts and feelings since he expects her to make him happy by believing that what he says is correct. The fact that he does not accept anything she believes will affect how she thinks about herself and the world around her. They have an expectation of how they should be and pass these expectations to their daughter. If the child does not do something according to the father's standards, she will be scolded, criticized, or both. Criticizing fathers will say that they are trying to teach their kids the right way to do things, but the truth is that they are very critical of their kids' personalities and styles. These fathers generally feel they are in the right since they pass these judgments onto their daughters.

Children who come from critical fathers may also have an expectation of what it means to love being a "good girl." If a child does anything deemed wrong for them, they may be considered "not a good girl," regardless if it is something small like losing something. The overall message that children who grow up with critical fathers receive is that being a "good girl" is a matter of living up to the father's expectations and standards.

Any deviation from that is considered a sign of failure. This may confuse the daughter, as she may comprehend that her father constantly criticizes her for being a good person, but she does not comprehend why it is so difficult to meet these expectations.

In most cases, when a child grows up with critical fathers between the age of 8 and 17, they become less autonomous in their thoughts and decisions. Suppose a father is extremely critical of his daughter. In that case, he is taking away her ability to make her own decisions regarding things that she believes in—because she will question them and wonder if they are really correct or not—which will cause more confusion for them than before.

A study in the *Journal of Adolescence* found that critical fathers strongly believe that "children should be taught almost everything about life." Because of this, they are very critical and judgmental of what their daughters think, do, and say. This may backfire on the daughter since she will try her best to do what her father wants and live up to his expectations. In fact, the daughters are judged by their fathers' standards of a "good girl"–whatever that may be. This will affect their overall life and instill a subconscious belief in them that they are not good enough, and they will try very hard to live up to their father's expectations.

4. Narcissistic Fathers

To a narcissistic father, the daughter is the ideal personification of his own ego and needs. The father is so wrapped up in his own needs and how he tries to live up to his idealized image of himself. In fact, he is so wrapped up in his own self that it is hard for him to see his daughter as being different from himself. It is also hard for him to see her as someone who would have any faults or problems with herself, no matter how different they may be from him. Therefore, to a narcissistic father, his daughter must always be the best. The daughter is considered either "good enough" or not at all. If a daughter is not the best, then he may attack her for not being good enough or "being a disappointment."

The feelings of the daughter will not be considered at all. The only thing that matters to the father is himself, and he does not actually care about his daughter's feelings. Whether she is feeling good or bad, happy or sad, it does not matter to him since his feelings matter most to him anyway. Narcissistic fathers are often called "intolerant" or "strict" regarding their daughters. They can either make her feel the pressure of being "the best" or feel unworthy of love.

If their daughters do not meet their expectations, they will somehow be punished by the father. This punishment may range from physical abuse or verbal abuse to complete neglect. In extreme cases, the father may even abandon his daughter, cut her off from the rest of the family, or he may disown her completely.

In severe cases, the daughter may sense that she is always fighting for something she does not actually deserve. The daughter will be left with a feeling of disappointment and guilt. She may feel like her father is disappointed in her because of how she "ought" to be, because of something she did wrong, or because she isn't living up to his idea of "what he raised her to be."

This will mess with how the daughter thinks about herself. She will begin to doubt herself and question her actions. She will also question why she isn't "good enough" to win her father's approval. In the end, the daughter may feel that if she cannot win her father's love, she will not be able to win anyone's love. This is another reason why a narcissistic father can negatively affect his daughter in a way that can last a lifetime.

This type of parental relationship is quite common, especially among politicians and other public figures who believe their image reflects their individual success.

5. Non-Involved Fathers

Instead of being active participants in their daughters' lives, non-involved fathers are more like spectators who observe their daughters' lives but are never really involved in them. A non-involved father will often not attend his daughter's school functions nor meet with her family, and he will not live by his daughter's rules or guidelines to do things. In fact, he may even teach his daughter that she is responsible for taking care of herself, as well as how to be on time, keep herself healthy, etc., in a way that seems like the daughter is an adult. The relationship between the father and daughter will be strained since the child does not know how to relate to her father normally since he is not really involved in her life.

Non-involved fathers may not even know that the child is aware that he isn't really involved with her life and may not have a clue that the child is feeling this way. This will make it seem like the child is trying to make her father understand, but he may not get what she is saying because he does not care about his daughter. It is true that fathers want their daughters to be independent, but there is a difference between independence and isolationism, and this father is taking it to the extreme by removing himself from his daughter's life completely.

The difference between non-involved fathers and physically absent fathers is that the physically absent fathers still support their daughters, but the chances of appearing in person because of certain circumstances are minimal, while the non-involved fathers may not support their daughters in any way. Also, non-involved fathers are the exact opposite of critical fathers; the critical father is very judgmental of his daughter, while the non-involved father doesn't care about his daughter in any respect.

A study in the *Journal of Adolescence* says that daughters whose fathers aren't involved in their lives will be very independent and won't talk about how they feel about things happening around them because they don't want to talk about it or think it's too personal. Instead, the daughters of non-involved fathers will try to talk about different personal things with their fathers, but it ends up being a big failure. The reason is that they don't feel like talking with their father in general and act like everything is fine;

The overall message that daughters of non-involved fathers receive is that they are on their own and should be more independent. Often, the message they receive from their father is that they need to make their own decisions rather than letting other people in their life tell them what to do. While this message may seem good at first, it ultimately creates an environment where the daughter thinks she can do things independently and not need anyone but herself. This will ultimately backfire on her and make her feel like she is not needed at all or part of their family, creating a strained relationship. The daughter will feel alone and unneeded, which is not good for anyone.

6. Distracted Fathers

These fathers will be so absorbed with something else that they often do not notice when their daughter may be having problems or feeling bad. They tend to be workaholics and perfectionists who are too busy, stressed out, and wrapped up in their own lives and problems to take the time to provide their daughters with hands-on guidance. These distracted fathers are generally not abusive or absent, but they do not have the time for their children. Their presence is there, but their minds are not, emotionally speaking.

Being distracted means that he is trying not to think about his daughter's needs and wants because he cannot handle them now. Because his mind is not with him, his daughter will begin to feel like she is not even a part of her father's family. The daughter will feel left out, isolated, insecure, and unneeded by her father. This will create a stage for daughters where they need to work harder to get their father's approval to feel wanted and accepted by him. Over time, the daughter will feel distant from her father and try to act like she doesn't need anything from him because she feels he cannot physically help her. Because of this, the relationship between the father and daughter will be strained at best, and the daughter will need to learn to take care of herself and be independent as an adult.

According to the book *Group Dynamics in Late Adolescence*, many people may feel they must pit their daughters against each other. Since these fathers are distracted and not involved with their daughters, they tend to think that this is how to get their daughter to grow up faster because she will have to learn things independently. In this situation, the father pressures his daughter to be more independent, and she will probably feel like he wants her to compete with her sister. In all actuality, fathers should help their daughters learn how to grow up and work through worries and challenges to develop a sense of competency. Fathers do not need to pit them against each other because they are trying to find out which one is better in their eyes.

Over time, these daughters may turn into very introverted individuals. They will rely on their friends and boyfriends for everything they want or need because they feel they cannot get it from their fathers. In addition, they will eventually be able to separate themselves from their family because they do not feel the need to be with them.

7. Competitive Fathers

These fathers see their daughters as threatening their authority or success and feel they are competing with them. They will constantly put down their daughter, say they are "better than her," and even try to make their daughter feel like she needs to work harder than everyone else to gain his approval and love. These competitive fathers need to dominate everyone. They feel that if someone else has something better, they can one-up them and show that they have something better, too. In their eyes, if the daughter is better than them, then they would not be better than anyone else in the family or the community. They want to be the best and do not want anyone to take that away from them. In addition, they will not allow the daughter to do anything to "get ahead" of them and do better in their eyes.

The connection between this type of father and emotional abandonment is very serious. The daughter will start to grow up and figure out that their father does not love them, making her feel unloved, unwanted, and unimportant. She will start to believe what she has been told about herself, about what she should be doing with her life—things that put her down and make her feel like less of a person. This may cause additional emotional problems for the daughter because she might hold these feelings against herself for as long as possible.

In addition to these problems, the daughter will not feel connected to her father because she will be forced to put him down to make herself feel better. This will create a rift between the father and daughter, ultimately making them drift apart. As a result, the relationship will be strained, and it will be very difficult for the two of them to communicate with each other in a positive way.

8. Indulgent Fathers

They are not physically abusive or absent but try too hard to make up for what is lacking in their daughter's life. They try so hard to be there and do everything for her, so she will never feel she is alone. Some of them overdo this so much that they spoil their daughters. They want them to have everything they cannot provide at the moment, so they give them as much money as possible and buy them things that may not fit into their lifestyle or are just not needed. They want their daughters to be happy, so they make sure they have everything they want.

Indulgent fathers spoil their daughters by buying them lavish presents and paying for everything, from getting their nails done to attending dances or other social occasions, as well as giving them money on a regular basis. Similar to the physically absent father, indulgent fathers are not physically absent because they are always in contact with their daughters, but like physically absent fathers, they tend to act very emotionally unattached towards their daughters. They pay more attention to her inter-personal relationships than her academic performance or career aspirations.

By purchasing extravagant gifts for their daughters, indulgent fathers are unintentionally communicating that they see them as objects to be bought and received rather than people to be loved and nurtured. Indulgent fathers may also expect to be showered with gratitude from their daughters, and when this is not the case, it can become a source of conflict, causing a great amount of distress for their daughters.

A study from the University of Pennsylvania found that almost one out of every three parents who say they spoil their kids are husbands and fathers. These fathers are the ones who struggle to make a living, and they want their children to feel special. Thus, they buy them gifts and spend their hard-earned money on their daughters. Their daughters see this as an act of love, but it really is not. Excessive gifting and overindulgence are signs that the father has issues with providing for his family and taking care of them in a way that makes them feel secure. It is also a sign that he does not know how to raise or nurture his daughter properly.

Spoiling children can be very damaging because when they grow older, they won't be able to recognize reality; they won't appreciate gifts or money because they will grow accustomed to having everything handed on a silver platter to them. As they grow older, they will be spoiled and will not learn to appreciate the things they have; they may feel that everyone around them has more than them, so they believe their lives aren't as good as theirs and will compare their lives to others. As a result, the spoiled child becomes unhappy and might even develop a social phobia, afraid to interact with other people because they feel others are judging them.

Most fathers want to be the best fathers they can be and provide their children with what they need to grow up into responsible adults and make something out of themselves. However, there is a fine line between fathering and spoiling your children; it is important to avoid crossing this line.

Being a father is a very big responsibility and should not be taken lightly. There are many ways to be an emotionally absent father, depending on what type of situation you were raised in and how that has shaped your life today. Each of these fathers will have a different way of raising their daughters, but all will cause the same damage. All the examples outlined above will cause emotional abandonment in their daughters, whether or not they realize it at the time.

CHAPTER 5: CAUSES OF FATHERS EMOTIONAL ABSENCE

J ust like anyone else, your father did not start out to plan abandon you. Unfortunately, when it comes to the ultimate goal of being a parent, people overlook many things and sometimes need to be made aware of them.

The reasons why all fathers are emotionally involved will be different, but what they have in common is those affected by their emotional absence.

The following are the most common causes of the father's emotional absence:

1. Mental Health Problems

According to the American Psychological Association, mental health problems can interfere with a person's ability to function properly. This can cause him to be emotionally absent from his daughter's life. Mental health problems can include depression, anxiety, and an eating disorder. In most cases, when it comes to mental health, the father is not even aware that he has a problem and will go on with his regular routine without realizing he is affecting the daughter's life.

Many different types of mental health problems cause an absent father, including:

a. Post-Traumatic Stress Disorder (PTSD)

It is a mental disorder triggered by experiencing or witnessing a terrifying event. Symptoms include flashbacks, nightmares, extreme anxiety, and uncontrollable thoughts about the traumatic event. This disorder can lead to the avoidance of many things and situations that trigger memories of the event. PTSD is common in men who were either soldiers or police officers, as they had to witness or experience violent acts that they were not able to prevent.

Everyone, regardless of ethnicity, nationality, culture, and age, is susceptible to developing PTSD. According to a report by the American Psychiatric Association, approximately 3.5% of U.S. adults are affected by PTSD each year. The estimated lifetime prevalence of PTSD in fathers is 4%. Women (13.7%) are more likely to develop PTSD than men (11.1%).

To further explain...

When a father has PTSD, he may go on with his life, pretending to be fine when he is really experiencing certain emotions eating away at him. Over time, he will become numb to what he is feeling, and from there, he will be unable to express how he actually feels. During this period, he will not be physically or emotionally present for his daughter. He will become extremely distant and will not communicate with anyone, including himself; he will not be able to explain any of the emotions that are causing him pain. Without realizing it, he will slowly start losing control over everything that is going on in his life and will eventually end up losing the thing that he loves the most: his family.

Those daughters whose fathers have PTSD can observe the effects of their father's mental health issues, but he will not perceive the impact of his actions on his daughter. He will not realize how he is going from the father she grew up with and can count on—a father who protects her, protects her heart, and keeps her safe from harm—to a father that is suddenly absent from her life. As a result, these fathers with PTSD tend not to care about their family as much as they should, or in some cases, at all. They tend to ignore their daughter's needs, become increasingly withdrawn and isolated from her life, and even worse: they may abuse their own children.

To keep the peace, the daughter will have to be very quiet and go with it. In some cases, they may act as though nothing is wrong, and in other cases, it may be unbearable. Whether they act out or not, they will have to learn how to cope with it all in the best way they know how: alone.

b. Anxiety Disorders

Those with anxiety may become distressed when they are in a certain situation because they believe something bad is going to happen, which impairs daily functioning. Those who suffer will show physical signs such as increased heart rate, sweating, trembling, shortness of breath, and muscle tension. They will also experience mental signs such as irritability, lack of concentration, fatigue, sleep problems, and restlessness. Because of these signs, the individual will become less productive in his daily life, negatively impacting his relationship with his daughter.

In the United States, Generalized Anxiety Disorder is one of the most prevalent mental disorders, according to the National Institute of Mental Health. In 2015, GAD affected more than 6.8 million adults (about 3.1% of the population) in the United States alone. Men are over two times more likely to be diagnosed with GAD than women. The prevalence of GAD in adults aged 45 and over is about 30% compared to 17% for those aged 18-44.

To further explain...

When a father has an anxiety disorder, it will be hard for him to be present in his daughter's life. He will be unable to handle the simplest of things and may even feel trapped in a situation or place he is unfamiliar with. To make matters worse, he will constantly be thinking the worst thoughts. He will start to believe there is no way out of his situation and that the outcome will be a disaster. He will also think of the worst possible outcomes, assume that everyone around him is always judging him, and assume that everyone hates him. As a result, he will feel anxious and stressed all of the time, which will negatively impact his life and his daughter's. This will cause him to distance himself from her, not care about her as much, and eventually even abuse his own children.

The daughter of a father with an anxiety disorder will be able to see the effects of his mental health problems, but he will not see how his actions are affecting her. He will not realize how she is going from being the daughter he loves and can count on—a daughter who loves and cares about him—to a daughter suddenly afraid of her own father. As a result, these fathers with anxiety tend not to care about their family as much as they should, or in some cases, at all. They tend to ignore their children's needs and become increasingly withdrawn from their family life.

To keep the peace and make sure nothing bad is going to happen, the daughter will have to be very quiet and go with it. In some cases, they may act as though nothing is wrong, and in other cases, it may be unbearable. Regardless of how they react—whether they act out or not—they will have to learn how to cope with it all on their own. They cannot expose the pain and hurt that their father has caused them because if they do, he will stop being present in their life completely.

c. Bipolar Disorders

Those with Bipolar Disorder go through mood changes that are severe and dramatic. During the manic phase, the person will have significantly elevated energy, optimism, and activity levels. In the depressed phase, the person will have significantly lower levels of energy and activity and more pessimism. These shifts can make it difficult to complete daily responsibilities, impacting the father's relationship with his daughter.

This affects 7.7 million adults aged 18 or older, according to the National Institute of Mental Health and the American Psychiatric Association. The estimated percentage of fathers with bipolar disorder is 1.9%.

To further explain...

Fathers with Bipolar Disorder will be unable to control the mood swings that are constantly happening within them. This father will go from being super happy to sad in the blink of an eye. He will go from being full of energy to having no energy at all. He will feel like nothing is going right in his life, and he will be overwhelmed with a sense of guilt. In this state, he will not be physically or emotionally present for his daughter. He cannot communicate with her or anyone around him. Instead, he will be all by himself in his own world. He will experience the pain that is within him, but he will not express it to anyone and will try his best to ignore it. He may even deny there is anything wrong with him at all.

The daughters of fathers with Bipolar Disorder will not fully understand what is actually happening within their fathers' minds. They will observe that he is absent and unwilling to participate in their lives. They will begin to feel lonely and sad, especially when they are around their fathers' mood swings. This will cause them to feel depressed, anxious, and sometimes even angry. The daughters will not be able to understand why their fathers are going through these mood swings or what is making them so sad.

To cope with this situation, they will act out to deal with the pain they are feeling. They may become irritable and angry with their fathers, causing a lot of tension in their relationships. There is also the chance that they may hurt themselves physically because they cannot express how they feel emotionally.

d. Obsessive-Compulsive Disorder

Obsessive-Compulsive Disorder (OCD) is a brain disorder that causes a person to have obsessive thoughts and compulsive actions. The individual will perform certain repetitive behaviors they feel are necessary to their daily life to relieve the anxiety and stress those thoughts are causing, causing him to neglect his daughter because he will be so focused on getting rid of the thoughts that are constantly affecting his mood.

A study completed by the Institute of Molecular Psychiatry at the University of Queensland, Australia, found that 4.9% of men and 7.1% of women between the ages of 17-94 suffer from OCD. The prevalence of OCD among fathers was 1.5% and 2.7% among daughters.

To further explain...

Fathers with obsessive-compulsive disorder will feel like they have to be in control of everything around them. They will be obsessed with the idea that everything has to be perfect and cannot do anything wrong–even the smallest things. As a result, they will constantly be checking and rechecking things they have done to ensure nothing is out of place or wrong. These fathers will get anxious when something goes wrong or when they become stressed about something small. They will feel like everything is a major issue and that everyone around them is looking at them, judging them for their mistakes. They will feel like everyone knows about their problems and that they are completely alone–even though people are around them. They will feel like life's challenges are too much to handle, so they will not be physically or emotionally present in their daughters' lives.

The daughters will not know how to deal with the anxiety and obsessiveness that is going on with their father. They will try their best to fix the situation by attempting to either change how they are acting or tell their father that everything is okay and that he does not need to worry about it. In some cases, they may feel like they need to control the situation to ensure everything is okay between them and their father. The daughters will ultimately believe that if they change and become more like what their fathers want them to be, they will feel better about themselves and their fathers will be more present in their lives again.

This can lead to a cycle of emotional abuse, where the daughter attempts to gain his love and affection by sacrificing herself to satisfy his needs. The daughter's behavior will lead her father to believe that she is perfect and that there is nothing wrong with her. The more the father is able to control her, the less anxious he will be and the more present he can be in her life. At the same time, the daughter will begin to feel helpless, angry, and depressed if she is unable to make him feel better about himself.

She may feel that something is wrong with her and that he does not love her because of it.

e. Dysthymia

At least two years of depressed mood accompanied by non-major depressive symptoms characterize dysthymia. The individual will have long-term low levels of energy, a pessimistic attitude, poor concentration and motivation, along with frequent feelings of hopelessness and guilt. They will feel like their life is not going anywhere or that they are unable to reach their fullest potential. They will feel unhappy about their current situation, which will cause them to isolate themselves from everyone and everything around them, especially their daughters.

A study completed by the National Institute of Mental Health found that 13.5% of men and 21.7% of women between the ages of 50-59 suffer from dysthymia. The prevalence of dysthymia among fathers was 4.1%.

To further explain...

The fathers that suffer from dysthymia will feel very low in energy and will not accomplish anything they set their mind to. They will feel like they have so much on their shoulders and that there is no way they will get everything done in time. They will try their best to take care of the family but end up getting extremely frustrated because there is not enough energy left over for them to do just that. They will feel like they cannot fit in everything that needs to be done, and because of this, they will start to feel hopeless about the situation. They will feel guilty for not living up to the promises and expectations laid out for them or the ones they set for themselves. This guilt will cause even more stress and anxiety since they are worried about disappointing their family. The fathers may start isolating themselves from the family because of their feelings of helplessness or from feeling like a burden to their family.

Their daughters will notice how distant their fathers are and attempt to connect with them to alleviate the stress he is experiencing. However, they will feel the need to remain in control and become angry with their daughters for trying to help. If them does not take the hint and stop asking fathers how they feel or about how the day has been, they will become more controlling toward her. Fathers will feel unrespected and probably think that everything they're doing is wrong or unimportant. They will imagine their self as a failure and a disappointment because family does not respect or appreciate all of the work has been done. They may try to be strict with daughters, maybe by blaming them for their own feelings of worthless.

The daughters will have no idea that the feeling experiencing because of their fathers isn't normal. This girls feels as if everything they do makes their fathers unhappy and upset, but without knowing the reason. They can try to talk about fathers' feelings and how difficult things are, but with no significant results. Daughters eventually believe that is better to go over because they are afraid to discover any signs that something might be wrong with them for not being able to make their fathers feel better.

These girls may get depressed and begin to feel like cannot do anything right. They could start to feel unable to get through everything because it feels too overwhelming and impossible. Maybe, in this situation, even taking self-care or living their everyday life could be too much and all of this stems from the development of guilt for not being able to relate their own parent.

Anyway, is important to understand the mental health issues are not easily identifiable. It can be hard for a father to understand how his actions can negatively impact his daughter. A father, or generally men, often finds it difficulty to seek professional help for these issues, maybe because of the lack of knowledge about them or due to erroneous beliefs transmitted by the society in which he lives. The more he isolates himself from his daughter, the more she will have no one to turn to for help. This will leave the daughter feeling alone, sad, and helpless. However, with the proper help, every father can learn to deal with his emotionally problems and be able to interact with his daughter more effectively.

2. Past Trauma

According to the National Council for Child Adolescent Psychiatry, past trauma is another factor that can affect a person's ability to parent in a healthy way. When a father has experienced some traumatic event in his life or abuse during his childhood, it can also affect his parenting skills. These types of events can be traumatic events such as sexual abuse, physical or verbal abuse, or other types of trauma that make a child feel less worthy than others. This can be a key factor in how he treats his children because of what he has learned from growing up this way and being exposed to a threatening environment. On the other hand, these types of events can also cause a person not to become attached to their children, and they may avoid the need to become a parent in the first place.

To further explain...

A study by the *"Journal of Family Psychology"* also showed that men who experienced early abuse or trauma were more likely to see their children as competitive or unloving when they were growing up. Other studies, however, have shown that children who are exposed to domestic violence are more likely to imitate their parents' behavior as adults. When kids are exposed to behavior like this and learn to do it for themselves, it can cause problems in their adult relationships with their kids. The kids will see their behavior as their own, not as their father's.

For example, instead of offering help to his daughter when she has a bad day or showing support through physical affection or love, the father is more likely to say her feelings are not valid or to "man up." This is because he has been in this situation before and has learned that the best way to deal with a traumatic event or trauma of any kind is to deal with it alone. He may have learned as a child that he could not rely on his family members, so he learned to be independent of them. In this sense, he cannot understand why his daughter should be treated any differently than he was as a child. He has not yet learned to rely on others and is inexperienced in showing affection to his daughter. This can cause the father to become more distant and angry with his daughter instead of accepting her as a person, loving her unconditionally, and helping her when she needs it most.

The father may also try to control or manipulate his daughter's emotions in order to make her feel bad about herself instead of learning to understand her. He may tell her she is being too sensitive when she cries, that she is overreacting, or that she does not have any reason to feel the way she does. He may also try to tell her how she should be feeling and how he would feel in certain situations, as if he knows exactly what his daughter is feeling at any given moment.

This can lead to issues between the two because the daughter will not understand why her father does not seem to compre-hend her and does not see it as a big deal. She will also feel like he is judging her and that she cannot talk to him about anything without being criticized or looked down upon for it. She will begin to feel like she does not know how to act or be herself around her father and will grow up feeling that everything is wrong with her. This further isolates the child and builds a wall between them, causing them to grow apart.

3. Work Pressure

Another thing that can contribute to the emotional absence of a father is work pressure. Fathers who feel overwhelmed by work or are constantly stressed may not have the time or emotional energy to build a relationship with their children and feel comfortable being around them. As the stress and exhaustion build up, the father will probably isolate himself from his family because he feels they are too much effort and that he cannot handle the additional responsibilities aside from his work. This will promote emotional absence, affecting the relationship between the father and his daughter.

To explain further...

A study revealed that people who are under a great deal of stress are more likely to experience negative emotions and have a diminished sense of life satisfaction. This can be an effect that a father feels when he cannot get away from work and is experiencing additional stress from being around his children for too long. The father may become very irritable when his daughter tries to get his attention and may snap at her or use impolite language or behavior towards her. He may also be more likely to ignore her or speak to her in a very cold or distant way, all because he cannot muster up enough strength and patience to deal with his daughter. He will therefore feel like she is a burden on him, making him feel that he needs some time away from the family, even if just for an hour or two. This will make him worried about his inability to support them, causing him to become withdrawn.

Work pressure is not only limited to fathers who are working full-time, but it can also include those with part-time jobs, free-lancers, or others who may struggle with money and bills. These individuals will likely feel less secure about their careers and may feel they do not have enough time to do something fun or cre-ative with their daughter because they need to complete more work, try to earn more money, or attend to other household responsibilities. This can affect their relationship, causing the father to feel even more stressed and tired than he already was, thus causing him to have less time to spend with his family, making him anxious about it.

This will also make him feel like he is not good enough or that she is better off without him, creating a separation between them. This will cause him to feel bad about himself and can result in him pushing his daughter away.

Most fathers want the best for their children and will go above and beyond what is expected of them to ensure their children are healthy and safe. They understand the importance of raising a child and work hard at it, but sometimes, life gets in the way and interferes with their parenting skills. They may not realize how much they are hurting their kids and they may feel like they have to give up their time with their kids because they can't find the energy to stay together.

The way fathers cope with these issues can be very different from how mothers cope with them. A father may feel like he or his parenting skills need to be better, and he is unable to provide for his family by himself. He may consider giving up on parenting because of this, feeling as if he will never be able to find a job again and, therefore, would never be able to support his family. He may also feel he does not have the motivation or desire anymore because of how tired he is feeling from trying so hard and being overwhelmed by it all. Some may even feel like they do not have the right to be around their children since they are not good enough.

4. Distractions

Fathers who have other interests or activities that engage them long-term or temporarily can be another reason for an emotional absence. This can include a job where your work requires you to be gone for long periods or hobbies that require a lot of time and effort. They may be unaware that they are behaving differently than their children because they are more engaged in the activity. The fun and excitement can make them forget their responsibilities or even their children. This can affect their relationship over time, causing them to become distant from each other and feel like they do not get along anymore.

To explain further...

A study showed that those who are highly involved in their hobbies or interests tend to believe that they have a better quality of life than those who are not. If they become involved in hobbies that require long-term dedication, there are many reasons why this might occur. They may have more ambitions and dreams, making it important for them to continue with it whether it is the right time for it or not. They may also get more fulfillment from the activity, feeling excited about doing it and inspired to continue doing it.

Alternately, they may be doing something new and exciting that they never imagined would occur, making them feel ecstatic and compelled to ensure they do not miss anything. Their enjoyment in these activities may cloud their judgment, causing them to think they can do them any time they want or that they do not need to be responsible because of how much fun it is. These thoughts will cause them to isolate themselves from their family, especially the children, or to be cold and distant towards them, causing them to feel abandoned and damaging the relationship between them and the father.

This will make him feel like he does not have enough time for his family or that he is not a good enough father. He may decide it is not worth the effort to try to be a good father since he does not enjoy it as much as he once did, causing him to feel frustrated with himself and stressed out about it, and the only way he can relieve some of this stress is to escape it all by focusing on his hobbies or work. It is the only thing that relieves him from being overwhelmed, and he does not want to lose his passion for it.

Hobbies and interests can be a good way to clear your head and get away from stressful situations. Some interests may even require you to spend time alone and be physically separated from others for you to do them. Sometimes, it is important for fathers to take some space to relieve the stress they have accumulated while being a father, but it is important that they make sure they put an end to it eventually so that they can get back into the family situation as soon as possible.

5. Separations or Divorce

Divorce can cause a lot of different circumstances that affect the relationship between a father and his daughter. Divorce is a difficult process for everyone involved, and many fathers may feel stressed by the situation or overwhelmed by how quickly it happens. They may feel hurt, angry, or guilty about the situation, making them neglect their responsibility as a father toward their daughter. Some may even be overwhelmed by the situation and feel alone, causing them to become careless about their child or the family situation.

To explain further...

Divorce's effects differ for everyone, and how they react to it may depend on various factors, including their personality and how they feel about the separation. A father may feel resentful toward his ex-wife, blaming her for the negative feelings he has, and this could affect his relationship with his daughter. He may begin to ignore her or lash out at her because of his emotions, taking it out on her since she is closer to him than anyone else is at the time. Alternatively, he may take it out on their daughter by being cold or neglecting her. This can also cause him to feel distant from her and as though he is not a good father, perhaps even causing him to feel guilty about the situation or to feel like he should have done more to prevent it.

A father may feel guilty about the situation as he has somehow failed everyone involved. He may feel he should have prevented the divorce or could have done more for his family. Having this sense of guilt will cause him to be distant from his daughter once again and make it even harder for her to relate to him in many situations. To get rid of this feeling, he may start blaming himself or second-guessing his actions, which can cause him to be cold and make her feel unloved and unwanted.

After a divorce, a father may go through a difficult time in his life and face many different complications and hardships. During these times, he may feel overwhelmed by the number and urgency of tasks that must be completed. This will make him want to run away from it all and try to escape all the problems for a while. He might want to spend time alone to gain some sense of pleasure or relief from his stress, which could cause him to neglect his daughter and the family situation. If he goes too far in withdrawing from the situation, it may cause many problems within the family, including arguments and tension among everyone involved.

A father may also feel angry towards his ex-wife during these difficult situations, feeling like he was wrongfully blamed for their separation. This feeling could cause him to be distant from his daughter and not spend time with her, or it could cause him to lash out and make her feel unloved and unwanted. A father may also be stressed about the situation, feeling overwhelmed by how quickly everything is changing in his life. He may start feeling disappointed in himself for failing at being a father, causing him to point out the things he feels are wrong with his parenting and to focus on them instead of all of the positives.

A father needs to realize that there is nothing wrong with him or his daughter during these situations and that the situation is usually in no way their fault. Also, the former spouses have to remember that they are both human and have flaws, but they are not responsible for fixing or preventing them from occurring. They are only responsible for the things that can be changed by themselves. If anything was wrong with them, it was in place before they even met, and their marriage or divorce would not have changed it. If there were issues to be fixed, they would have been altered by the family going forward throughout their lives together as a family unit.

6. Lack of Positive Role Models

Fathers who lacked positive father figures in their childhood may lack guidance in building healthy and emotionally satisfying relationships with their children. This may be the result of their father physically or emotionally leaving at an early age, or it may be a result of their father being emotionally or physically abusive. As adults, they may find they are not as well-versed in learning how to build healthy relationships with their daughters.

To explain further...

According to the National Fatherhood Initiative, a father figure is "a positive male role model in a young person's life." This can include their own father, stepfathers, grandfathers, friends, or family members. A positive father figure will not only help shape his perspective on what is right and wrong but guide him on how to treat others, how to build his relationship with his children, and how to treat his own daughters.

A positive relationship with his father can also help them feel more confident when dealing with their own children. It can help them feel like they have a better grasp on what is expected of them in an adult relationship and make them more at ease in their role as a parent. A positive relationship with their father may also help them feel confident in other male relationships.

Without this type of understanding, he may feel more confused and unsure of what kind of role he should be trying to model for his daughter. He may not be aware of how to communicate with his daughter in a way that would build their relationship positively. He may also not know how to care for his daughter properly and understand her emotional needs while helping her grow up as an adult. Additionally, a lack of good father role models can lead a father to be more passive in his own relationships, leading him to be more passive in other aspects of his life. A passive father may feel more awkward trying to be a parent. He may feel uncomfortable in situations where he has to deal with his daughter or any other people or situations. This can cause him to withdraw from the situation or become less involved with his daughter, which will eventually cause the relationship between them to stagnate and deteriorate.

7. Lack of Awareness

Some fathers do not realize how important it is to be emotionally present in the relationship and establish an emotionally engaged relationship with their daughter. They are either unaware of their emotional absence, or they do not feel it is the right time to start emotionally engaging with their children. They do not see the importance of emotionally engaging with their children or may not feel it is necessary.

To explain further...

It has also been shown in research studies that fathers tend not to take an active part in raising their children because they do not want to overburden themselves or they feel it is not their job or responsibility. They may believe they lack the authority to do so or that their children are old enough to care for themselves or be raised by their mothers. They might feel like their wives have enough responsibility for caring for the household and raising the children, so they should bear the burden of parenting alone. They may also have gotten tired and discouraged from the constant effort required to maintain an emotionally engaged relationship with their daughter. Thus, they have stopped trying or even wanting to do it. They may feel like it is too much for them or that they no longer have the energy for it, so instead, they choose to stay detached from them. Even if they decide to be emotionally engaged with their children, they feel as if their daughter is too old or too mature to need them anymore, causing them to feel as if they are not needed and that they should remove themselves from the situation completely.

On the other hand, they have had problems emotionally engaging in the past, causing them to shut it down completely out of fear that they will hurt their relationship with their daughter again if they get close to them. They may fear they will be unable to deal with the stress of being emotionally engaged if something goes wrong, and it will cause them to end up more distant from their daughter than before, not knowing how to get closer. Having this fear can make them feel restless and anxious about trying it again in the future, causing an emotional absence from their daughter.

8. Cultural and Societal Factors

How fathers are treated by society is a major factor affecting family dynamics. Society affects the father's ability to be there for his family, especially regarding the stereotypes society imposes on fathers. People may have certain ideas or expectations about fathers and how they should be living their lives, causing those who do not fit into certain stereotypes to feel like they are not good enough.

To further explain...

There are certain expectations of fathers in every culture and society, which sometimes do not accurately show how fathers feel or what they actually want to do with their families. The father may feel like he has to conform to these expectations to please others or due to the pressure that society is putting on him to be a certain way to be accepted. He may be trying to fulfill these expectations, but his situation may need to match the way that these expectations are set.

A good example of this includes stay-at-home fathers. These types of fathers are becoming more and more common, but they still face many challenges when trying to provide for their families and raise their children. Their lives are filled with constant stigma and criticism from others, who think that they do not know enough about parenting or that they should be the ones providing for their family financially rather than staying at home. This always puts pressure on them, causing them to feel as if they are not good enough to be a good father. Even if they are doing a great job, they may still feel as if they are not good enough to provide for their family because of the societal pressures pushing and pulling at them.

Men are traditionally seen as the ones who are supposed to be there for their families, but this does not have to be so. Men can take on many different roles in society and still be good enough as a father. Fathers can fulfill their parental responsibilities in various ways, whether by being stay-at-home dads or taking on a part-time job and working when needed. There is no one way that fathers should live their lives. They are just human beings trying their best and deserve to be treated accordingly.

Stigma is also placed on single fathers, who are usually considered bad parents because they do not have a wife to help them raise the children. There is no reason why this should be seen as a negative thing; it's just how society works and how people expect things to work. The father may feel like he is not good enough for the child or that he will never be able to provide for his family the way that it needs or wants to be provided for. This can cause him to feel bad about himself, especially if he does not have anyone to help support or encourage him through this difficult time.

Any father, whether it be biological or adoptive, is allowed to love their child regardless of gender or the reason why they are raising their child. They can still provide for their family and are just as good of a parent as any other parent. They should be treated with courtesy and respect and never be criticized for their parenting choices. The only thing that matters is that they provide for the needs of their family in the best way they can.

There are several reasons why a father cannot provide the emotional support they should provide their daughter. Regardless of why a father cannot provide for his daughter's emotional needs, serious consequences can follow. Despite this, it is essential to remember that they are human beings attempting to do their best. Whether from past situations or stressors within their everyday life, they are still important people to their daughters and should not be pushed aside because of these issues. Knowing and understanding these situations can greatly benefit you as a daughter and give you the ability to better understand why they are the way they are. This can make it easier for you to communicate with them and reach out to them when you need emotional support.

PART 3 - BUILDING A NEW HEALTHY AND REALISTIC RELATIONSHIP WITH YOUR FATHER

CHAPTER 6: RECONSIDERING THE FATHER FIGURE

E very girl has a "father picture" in her mind that is based on her experiences with her father. This picture involves expectations and beliefs regarding him and what she "thinks" he should have been like. Your father figure will affect how you live the rest of your life. How you see this image–or how you perceive it—will continuously change as you age. Your views and opinions about your dad are now being challenged by experience and maturity, so it's only natural for some confusion to come up.

Understanding Your Emotionally Absent Father Figure

Your father figure is far from what you may have believed about him as a child. He may have been so wrapped up in his own problems that he did not pay attention to your needs, or he may have been emotionally unavailable because of his personal problems. Regardless of the reason, it is essential to comprehend why your father has become emotionally distant. This is crucial so that you can realize what it is about your relationship with him currently causing you pain and, most importantly, what you can do about it.

Take time to understand what drives him to behave the way he does. Often, his behavior is caused by the same factors that affect you. He has fears and insecurities, and he may have dealt with or is still dealing with problems that affect him emotionally. Maybe he has psychological problems; maybe he carries guilt, fear, or shame; or maybe he is angry and bitter. He may be going through a hard time in his life and feels powerless to change it. Or maybe he is just so preoccupied with his own life that it also seems too difficult for him to pay attention to you. Whatever the reason, he is still your father figure, and it's up to you to try and make a relationship with him.

Empathy for Your Dad

Remember that we are all human beings—even your father. If you understand how fallible people can be, you can forgive them for their mistakes. As mentioned earlier, it's important that you see your dad as a real person and recognize that he has feelings, too. He has faults and weaknesses, just as everyone else does. No one is perfect; however, our flaws make us human. Just as excessive pressure can cause a small crack to become a full-blown fracture, a little disappointment can become something much bigger. It's better to try to understand instead of judging. Not only will this help you have a more positive outlook on life, but it will also help you accept reality and make better choices. After all, knowing where your dad is coming from will be easier to understand him.

When you feel empathy for your father, it allows you to recognize that you are not alone in your pain and that he is struggling as well. It can be a very powerful feeling to realize that both of you are in the same situation–something neither of you planned for or wanted. This can help both of you realize the importance of becoming a whole person and growing (or healing) together. It's an experience that neither of you wanted or planned for, but it can help you change the way you see each other. Empathy is not only important when it comes to your father; it also applies to yourself because for you to heal and grow, your father needs healing and growth.

Other Ways to Understand Your Father Figure

Here are some other ways to understand your father, or anyone, for that matter:

1. If you can't see it, confront it.

There is something about your father that you don't understand. Ask him about the situation and try to find out why he may have acted the way he did. Be sure not to take his answers at face value because they will be an attempt to justify his behavior. Even if this needs to be fixed, keep trying until you find out what isn't being said. This is an important step in saving your relationship with your father. If you don't confront him and try to understand the situation, you will be doing yourself a disservice. Not only will this keep you from understanding him, but it will also keep you from seeing the situations in which you act like him. Ignoring the problem will add more pain and anger to the relationship.

Questions like:

- "Why did you do that?"

- "What made you so angry?"

- "What has been going on inside you that has made you act this way?"

- "Why did you hurt me?"

- "Why do I feel this way?"

- "Can we work together to fix what's wrong?"

These questions are better than just looking at the situation and saying, "You are the worst person I've ever known! Why do you treat me like this?" It will help you see what he is hiding and why he is doing this to you. Once you see it, you can disagree with his actions and figure out what he feels is causing him to treat you like this. This will also help you understand better what he is going through.

Through this process, you can find out why he has been acting the way he does and his reasons for doing so. If he refuses to discuss the situation and take responsibility for his actions, you have taken a step toward healing because you have attempted to determine what is happening. The only reason this is a step towards healing is because of your attempt at achieving understanding and reaching a consensus.

But remember that you might not get the answers you need. Maybe your father does not want to talk about it and is stubborn, or maybe he is just trying to find a way out of having to deal with his problems. Either way, you are making a move in the right direction. It's important that you keep going until you have exhausted all options and discovered everything you can to understand where he is coming from.

2. Reflect on Expectations and Disappointments

Daughters of emotionally absent fathers often have unrealistic expectations of their fathers because, without realizing it, they have defined their fathers' love as something that had to be earned. Their views on what their father's love should be like were formed as they matured and realized that they didn't receive the same level of attention or affection that other children received from their fathers. These things made them feel alone in the world, which ultimately caused an expectation that their father should come to them and show a level of care and affection toward them, similar to how they are seen by others who are not related to them. As time passed and their fathers did not live up to their expectations, these daughters suffered many disappointments that led to anger, frustration, hurt, and confusion.

Reflecting on these expectations and disappointments can help you better understand your emotions and work to accept the reality of what happened to you in the past.

How to do this?

Step 1: Write Down Your Expectations

The first step is to record your expectations by responding to the questions below.

Q: What do I expect from my father?

A: I want my father to _____
(something that you want from your father like: be romantic,

be protective, be attentive, etc. As long as it is something that would make your relationship with your father more meaningful and fulfilling.)

Q: What are the reasons behind my expectation?

A   **:**

_____(explanation about why you want what you want from your father. For example, if you expect your father to be "romantic," it is important that you explain why this is such an important quality. It could be because you feel unloved and unaccepted by your father or fantasize about a romantic hero type of father. Whatever the reason is, make sure you identify it to get a clearer picture of why this is important to you.)

Q: Are my expectations realistic?

A: YES___ NO___ (if your answer is yes, great! If not, try to go back and think about what happened in the past that led to the way things are today. Think about how your father has hurt you and ask yourself if having unrealistic expectations would make your life even more painful.)

Q: If my expectations are not realistic, what is the reality behind them?

A: _____ (this is a reality check on what the reality of the situation is. Make sure to think back to everything that has happened in your life with your father and come up with an honest answer as to why you hold certain unrealistic expectations.)

Q: How do I feel when I have these expectations?

A   **:**

_____

(This question is where you get to express all of your emotions that you have been holding onto. Writing down your expectations and then reflecting on their reasons is a great way to get your emotions out into the open. Getting these feelings out into the open this way will help you feel less alone and more in control of your life.)

Step 2: Write Down Disappointments

The next step is to write down disappointments. This part is similar to the first step because you are still defining your expectations of your father, but now you add disappointment.

Q: What am I disappointed about my father?

A   **:**

_____

(list all of the disappointments that you are holding onto. This can include things such as: not paying attention to me, being short with me, not being loving and attentive, etc.)

Q: Am I right in being disappointed in my father?

A: YES___ NO___ (if your answer is yes, great! If not, try to go back and think about what happened in the past and draw an honest conclusion on whether or not you should have these feelings toward him.)

Q: How do I feel when I am disappointed with my father?

A   :

_____

(This question is where you get to express all of your emotions that you have been holding onto. It is important to note that these emotions can be intense and difficult to manage, especially if the disappointment stems from an event that occurred a long time ago. In this situation, the best course of action is to write down your emotions and then release them.)

Step 3: Get the Facts

The next step is to ask your father the questions you have wanted answers to. Before asking these questions, it is important to think about what you want from your father. Do you expect him to give you a full breakdown of every detail of his life? Do you expect him to be as open and honest as possible? Or do you want him to answer "yes" or "no" and leave it at that?

Most daughters trying to get answers from a distant father have one thing in common: they want the truth. To feel satisfied, they will need their fathers' full honesty and would prefer not to have any secrets between them. So, if your father holds back or is reluctant to give you the answers you are looking for, it is important to ask him why he chooses to be closed off in this way. If necessary, ask him questions anyway and give him the space and time he needs to express himself.

The answers you get from your father will answer all of your previous questions but may also open up an array of other questions you had not even thought about before. These additional questions are best dealt with after the fact. The goal at this point is to have a proper conversation with your father and get answers as opposed to getting information.

Step 4: Accept the Reality of Your Existing Relationship With Your Father

The final step is to accept and embrace the existing relationship that you have with your father. This is not an easy task, and it might even be painful, but it is necessary. There comes a point in every daughter's life when she must accept and embrace the truth of how things are now. This can be very difficult if you were expecting more from your father, but remember that he, too, has his feelings, history, and limitations. He, too, is human, and he, too, will make mistakes. And, even though you might not like how your father is, it is important to remember that he is still a father, and he is still there for you.

This process can be very rewarding if you put the work into it. It forces you to accept both the good and bad qualities of your relationship with your father while allowing you to express yourself healthily. If used properly, this process can alter your perceptions of him in a positive way and help heal any wounds that have been uncovered along the way.

The first few times that you do this exercise can be very hard. However, as time goes on and you reflect upon the things that your father has done in your life, it will become easier and more comfortable. You will find that this exercise is an excellent tool for healing your wounds, and it will help you feel closer to the father figure you have always wanted.

What to Expect When Doing This Exercise:

- This exercise can be uncomfortable for both parties if your father does not like being asked questions about his past or his feelings in general. This is normal.

- You will want to devote as much time as possible to this exercise because you want the process to be very thorough, and you do not want it to be rushed.

- Trying to write down all of your feelings is normal during the course of this exercise for many daughters, but if it becomes too difficult for you, or if it feels that writing down all of your feelings is actually causing more distress than good, then try writing down only some of them and approaching the rest in a later session if you feel up to doing so.

- You may find yourself being very emotional during the course of this exercise. This is normal.

- You might want to write down your questions in advance. This will make it easier to ask your questions and can also act as a reminder to you when your mind is wandering too far or if you feel like giving up and not asking any questions at all.

3. Think About Whom You Are Communicating With

Communicating with your father, especially those who were emotionally absent, is much different from communicating with others. You must keep in mind that your feelings are unique to you, and your father will not always understand your feelings because he may have had a different upbringing. You must realize that if you are communicating with someone who is emotionally unavailable, it is important to express yourself on an emotional level.

How to do this?

Step 1: Don't React to Hurtful Comments

Your father may say something that is emotionally hurtful to you. In this situation, it is important not to react emotionally but to think about what he is trying to say. You may think he is being mean or critical when he is trying to show you that he cares and wants you to make better decisions with your life. It may help if you tell yourself that you are overreacting because your father has never been able to express himself like this before. Tell yourself that it was difficult for him to share his feelings with you this way and understand the message behind his words. Repeat back to yourself his exact words and ask him to clarify what he means by saying this. If you listen to him, you could find something you have in common instead of focusing on the hurtful words.

Step 2: Think About His Point of View

Think about your father's point of view. You may be upset but try to understand why he said what he said. Think about how a situation might be seen from his side. Always keep in mind that your feelings are unique and special to you, and your father does not always understand how this situation impacts your life because he had a different upbringing than you did. Evaluate what your father is trying to say and see if there are any underlying emotions and meanings behind his hurtful words.

Try to find out what he is attempting to express or accomplish by saying the things that he says. If you can do this, try your best to understand the message behind his hurtful words and try to help him express his feelings in a way that is healthy for both of you.

Step 3: Learn to Take Personal Responsibility

When you are dealing with your father, you must learn to take personal responsibility for your actions and decisions. You cannot expect him to understand or want to understand every aspect of your life, and this is okay. As long as you are making healthy decisions based on the information you have and are taking care of yourself, then it is okay for him not to understand everything about your life. He can be there for you when he feels it is necessary, and he can offer advice when he thinks it will help, but you must take responsibility for your feelings and decisions.

It is important to remember that you will not always be on the same page as your father. He, too, has his emotions, and he will make mistakes from time to time. This does not mean that one of you is right and the other is wrong; it means that both of you have different perspectives. Your perspective might be healthier for you, but his perspective might be healthier for him. It is essential to realize that no matter how much you love someone, they will never make all of your decisions or fully comprehend your life.

By reconsidering your father figure, you will help yourself develop emotional awareness and self-understanding to aid in healing. In addition, it can help you get rid of anger, resentment, and disappointment and accept the past so you can focus on the present and future. You need to remember that even though your father may have hurt your feelings with his actions or words, that does not mean that he did not care about you. He was doing the best he could based on his limited experiences and knowledge of life. But it does not give your father a "free pass" for all of his wrongdoings or neglect against you; however, it can help you accept those wrongdoings and neglects because it allows you to see them in a different light.

CHAPTER 7: NEW WAYS TO CONNECT WITH YOUR FATHER

Once you have understood your father, developed empathy for him, and acknowledged what he has been through, you will be able to see the world in a different light. It opens up the realization that life is not always about you or your father and his problems. People are more than their mistakes; they are more than their own issues and deserve compassion and a chance to start over. Knowing how much pain you have caused others around you, it's time to change how you see them and yourself.

Once you have taken time to realize that your father is human like everyone else and has a story of his own, you will be more willing and open to change your perceptions about him. You can also forgive your father for all he has done wrong and for what he could not do right for him to be a part of your life growing up. With this new understanding and perspective, you will be able to develop a new relationship with your father.

Finding New Ways to Connect With the Emotionally Absent Father

There are numerous ways to establish a new, realistic, and healthy relationship with your father, including:

1. Find New Ways to Communicate

Since you have already discovered what does not work in your relationship with your father, it is time to find out what does work. One of the biggest mistakes daughters make is trying to communicate with their fathers in the same way they have in the past. For instance, if you have always felt ignored and unimportant, talking about your problems with him will never work because he doesn't care. So, you will need to find new ways to communicate and express yourself with him.

The following suggestions are intended to help you communicate with your father more effectively:

a. Write a Letter

Consider writing your father a letter about how you feel. The purpose of this is to describe how you feel about your relationship with him and what you need to rebuild your relationship.

He might not respond or even open the letter, but it will make you feel better and can also be helpful in letting go of all the negative feelings you have kept inside for so long.

You may want to write down all of your feelings and thoughts on paper before sending the letter so it doesn't come out as one big rant but instead is clear and concise. Start with "Dear Dad," and then write down everything you want to tell him.

For example, you might write, "I feel like I have never been able to express myself to you, so I have decided to write down how I feel." You can add other details or feel as though you want to explain everything from the beginning and still end up saying what you want to say without going on too long or breaking any of the rules. Also, if you want to express your feelings through a letter, try to make sure you include every feeling or thought that comes up so he can see them clearly.

The next time you write a letter to your father, try to include more details and tell him about the things that are important to you. You might tell him about your friend's problems, how tired you are at work, or how much you miss him. Again, it's best to think everything through and be as honest as possible with yourself when writing down something you know will get a response from your father.

Writing letters can also help you express your feelings without confronting him in person immediately. This can be helpful if your father is emotionally unavailable and unable to handle a lot of emotion in one setting. As you write him a letter, you can also remind yourself that you are doing it for yourself because it is not a one-sided relationship. It gives you another chance to communicate with him and tell him what's happening in your life.

b. Active Listening

Active listening is a form of communication in which the listener actively seeks to comprehend the meaning and intent behind the words spoken by another person. It demands active participation in the communication process. It is important in communication because it keeps you engaged with your father in a positive manner. Additionally, it makes your father feel valued and heard. This ability is the basis of any successful conversation and will help you greatly in any type of conversation with your father.

How to do this?

Step 1: Be Fully Present

Active listening necessitates total engagement in the conversation. This allows you to concentrate on the speaker. Being present involves listening with all of your senses (sight, hearing, etc.) and giving the speaker your undivided attention. Put away your cell phone, ignore distractions, refrain from daydreaming, and silence your internal dialogue. Concentrate on your father's words and try to understand the meaning behind them. This will also help you control how you react to what he is saying and make it easier to understand the message.

Step 2: Pay Attention to Your Non-Verbal Cues

The way you react to what he says can set him up for the conversation. To show your father that you're truly tuned in, use open, non-threatening body language like nodding, shaking your head, and smiling, and verbal cues like **"uh-huh"** and **"okay."** He should feel there is no risk in telling you anything and that you will not take it wrong. If he says something offensive, take a deep breath and ignore it because it may not be directed at you.

Step 3: Paraphrase and Clarify

This step is very important in active listening. After your father says something, repeat his statement to him using your own words so he can make sure that you understand what he is trying to say. Clarify what you heard by asking questions so you understand his message better.

For example, ask him if he feels hurt or misunderstood because of something that someone said or did. This will show him that you are listening and caring about what he is saying and feeling. You can also give him a chance to clarify what he means by asking specific questions about your interpretation of his message. This step is very helpful because it keeps the conversation on track and allows both parties to express their thoughts and feelings clearly.

Step 4: Give Feedback and Share Thoughts

Once you feel like you understand what he is saying, give your father feedback. Provide advice or ask open-ended questions, like **"what do you think should be done about this?"** This way, he will know that he has been heard and understood. You can also share your thoughts or reactions to what he said to show him that you care about his thoughts and feelings. Sharing your thoughts is important because it helps him realize that you are truly listening to what he is saying and that you have taken the time to understand his point of view.

Step 5: Take Responsibility and Respect Your Father's Feelings

This is the final step in active listening. Once you have listened to your father and given him feedback, show him that you respect his feelings or suggestions by accepting or refusing to accept what he said. If you don't agree with something, give him an explanation or a reason why you prefer your own way instead of his. You can also suggest how he might do things differently to show that you take the situation seriously and care about his feelings. If you do not agree with what he said, sometimes it is okay to disagree. This shows that you are trying to fully understand and appreciate his point of view while also taking your own into consideration.

Active listening is important because it gives you a chance to understand his core beliefs, opinions, and feelings. This will allow both of you to express yourselves freely and respectfully without becoming confused or angry.

c. Use "I" messages

"I-messages" reflect the sender's feelings and observations rather than direct accusations or criticisms of another person. When you use I-messages, you are describing your own thoughts or feelings and what you want to do about them. These statements are typically non-threatening and nonjudgmental. I-messages stand in contrast to You-messages, which blame or accuse the other person. This will help you and your father in your communication by making it easier to express your thoughts and feelings and take the time to understand him.

How to do this?

Step 1: Identify Your Feelings

Be honest with yourself about your true feelings and thoughts. Come up with a specific statement describing your concerns and how you feel to provide clarity every time you communicate with your father. This will make the conversation less threatening and allow you to express what is really important to both of you.

For example, you might say, **"I'm feeling confused because I don't understand what you mean by..."** or **"I feel sad when I think about..."** This step is very important because it allows you to effectively communicate what you're thinking and feeling in the clearest possible way. It also helps you gain clarity on the situation so the next step can be taken. This step is also important because it helps you express your true feelings.

Step 2: Identify Your Concerns

Once you have identified what you're feeling and how you feel, be clear on why you feel this way. For example, why do you feel sad? If you have a valid concern, explain it by saying, **"I'm feeling sad because..."** or **"I don't know what to do about..."** This step is necessary because sometimes people express their true feelings but do not take the time to explain the underlying reason for their concerns. It also helps reassure him by giving him a clear understanding of the situation.

Step 3: Communicate Your Feelings and Concerns Clearly and Non-Judgmentally

Use I-messages to express yourself. To do this, take responsibility for your feelings by saying **"I feel..."** or **"I'm feeling..."**

instead of **"You make me feel..."** This shows that you are ready to accept any consequences of the situation. It also helps your father understand what you feel since he will know that it's not something that came out of nowhere in the conversation.

For example, you might say, **"When you talk about President Bush like this, I feel like you don't respect my opinion,"** or **"When you call me out of my full name, I feel like you're insulting me, and I want to hit back at you."** This step is very important because it shows your father that you are aware of what is going on and that you truly mean what you are saying. It also helps him understand your feelings better.

Step 4: Be Specific

This step is very important because it makes sure that both parties are clear about the intention of the message being conveyed. If there are unresolved issues in the conversation, this step will help them get to the root of the problem.

For example, if your father says, **"You work too hard,"** but he means, **"I'm too old-fashioned, and I'm afraid that your job will take you away from me,"** you can ask him to clarify or explain his statement. This will also help him feel closer to you because of the time it took to really understand each other.

Making these clear and effective I-messages can help in all types of conflict, including family conflicts. However, it is especially useful in conflict situations like the one that you find yourself in with your father. Once you have identified your feeling and concerns, you can show him how to understand what you mean. Being specific about what you're feeling will help establish clearer communication between the two of you without fear of judgment or confusion. It also allows you to be clearer about what you want from him and what you expect from him in terms of the situation.

d. Controlled Sharing

This type of communication makes use of all the previous forms to achieve a more effective outcome. It is essential to note that this form is not intended for individuals who have difficulty expressing their true feelings and thoughts. This is because people who do not wish to share these things with another person are able to easily identify this form. When you use controlled sharing, you allow your father to know what you're feeling and thinking, but you also keep the control and power in your hands. This means that you can stop whenever you want if you do not feel comfortable saying what you're thinking. It also gives your father the feeling that he is in control of the situation, which helps build trust and understanding.

How to do this?

Step 1: Identify Your Feelings and Thoughts

This step is similar to the previous one but is even more important. In this step, you must be honest with yourself about your true feelings and thoughts. This will show that you are willing to take the time to understand what is really important to your father and yourself.

For example, you might say, **"I am feeling angry when I think about..."** or **"When I think about..."** These statements are very informative because they will help show that you are aware of what is going on and that you truly mean what you say. It also helps your father better understand how he should handle the situation so that it can be addressed effectively in future conversations.

Step 2: Control Your Emotions

In this step, you control your emotions so they do not get in the way of the conversation. This step is necessary because some people are easily affected by their emotions and may take things out of proportion. Using controlled sharing allows you to think more clearly about what to say and how to express it so that you won't say something hurtful, which could be very harmful in future conversations.

For example, if you feel shy when talking to your father, you can say something like, **"OK, I want to tell you this, but I feel shy right now,"** or **"I can't say it, but will you please just listen?"** This shows that your feelings will not get in the way of the conversation. It also enables you to express yourself more easily because saying why you feel the way you do can be very difficult. Putting a stop to those emotions is like removing a barrier that may prevent you from saying what you mean, so keeping things like this to yourself is essential when using controlled sharing.

Step 3: State Your Feelings and Concerns Clearly

Controlled sharing enables you to express yourself more easily by removing the emotional barrier. This means you can be more specific about what is important to you, which is very important in effective communication. In this step, you can take your time when saying what bothers you, but don't make a long-winded speech about the situation because sudden changes in the conversation can make your father lose interest. You should also use emotional words generously so that your father can understand your feelings and how he should handle the situation.

For example, you might say, **"I'm angry when you say that..."** or **"This makes me feel bad because..."** This shows that you have taken the time to understand what is really important to your father and yourself. It also shows that you are willing to be open about these issues and clearly mean what you say.

Step 4: Control Your Behaviors

This is a crucial step because it demonstrates your willingness to take the time to control your behavior around your father. When you can remain calm, it is much easier for others to relax and listen. Using controlled sharing also teaches your father how he should act in a given situation to be more effective in his approach.

For example, you might say, "**I feel hostile when...**" or "**This makes me feel like....**" This shows that you want to express your feelings but does not mean you must take over speaking in the conversation. It also helps him understand the behavior, improving his ability to handle future situations effectively.

Step 5: Clarify What You Want

Using controlled sharing also enables you to clarify what you want from your father so that there is no confusion about handling future conversations. Using this form of communication also helps build trust and understanding, which can only help the relationship between the two of you. In this step, you can state exactly what will make your father happy. Without knowing what is expected, it's hard for him to know how he should respond.

For example, you might say, **"I want things to go back to normal now,"** or **"I want us to be the same again."** This statement shows that you are willing to consider what your father wants and needs right now. It also shows that you are willing to compromise on what you want so that the two of you can agree on a future course of action.

Step 6: Let Your Father Respond

Give your father a chance to respond to what you have just said. This will help the two of you come to a better understanding of how the other one feels. In this step, it is very important that you refrain from taking over speaking in the conversation. This technique shows respect by letting others speak and having an attitude that says, "I'm ready to listen." This shows that you are not just waiting for a chance to get your own words out but are also really interested in what your father has to say. It also helps you better understand how your father will handle future situations because he will probably consider what you have said. In return, he can be more open to ideas, making it easier for him to understand the situation.

For example, you might say, **"I'm listening,"** or **"That's very interesting,"** or **"Tell me more about how you feel."**

Step 7: Review and Summarize

Summarizing what was said in the conversation helps your father assess his effectiveness at speaking to you. It also lets him know that what he has said has been understood, which gives him one less thing to worry about. This step is important because it shows that he can talk to you without worrying about repeating his words to others. It also shows that you are willing to make an effort to listen to what he has to say and that you respect that effort.

For example, you might say, **"So, what I'm hearing is..."** or **"I understand how you feel,"** or **"Thanks for talking about this with me. I appreciate it."**

Controlled sharing is also essential because it demonstrates that you are accountable for your own emotions and actions. It is a very effective communication skill that many people can use. This form of communication is best suited for long conversations, so a great deal of content can be communicated to others. Some topics may not be suitable for this technique because they require other forms of communication, like solution-focused language or storytelling.

Communication is complicated because there are so many different ways to do it, but the purpose of communication is to be understood by the other person. Having communication with your father, you should have a greater understanding of the other person and how he feels. If you are open to hearing what your father has to say and being honest about your feelings and thoughts, you should be able to communicate both your thoughts and feelings successfully. By communicating with your father, you can improve how you communicate with him and handle future situations. Communication is complicated, but when it is done right, it can be very effective.

2. Develop New Activities Together

Spending time with a person without having to talk about your problems is a great way to build a new relationship with your father. Try working on projects together that you both enjoy. This is an excellent way to make your father feel important and it gives you new things to do together. These activities aim to find new ways for you and your father to interact with each other in a healthy way that feels authentic and honest.

The following are some suggestions for activities that you might want to participate in with your father:

• Find New Hobbies or Interests Together

Finding new hobbies or interests can be very helpful for you and your father to enjoy your time together. When you select a hobby, try to find activities that will help you both learn something new and expose you to new ideas. You might try learning a musical instrument together or reading the same books. This will help you both grow and meet new people. Having something new in your life to be interested in will help you feel more fulfilled and better understand the world around you.

By choosing new activities, you are showing your father that you are willing to try new things together. It is important for the two of you to find things you can enjoy together so that you will continue to spend time doing them regularly. For example, if your father likes playing golf, try to find more activities with him where he can golf. This will help with maintaining a healthy relationship with your father because it shows that you are not just focused on yourself but also on what he wants and needs. This will show him that he can still have a bond with you despite everything that has happened in the past.

- **Take a Trip Together**

If there is an opportunity for you and your father to go on vacation together, make sure that you take it and use this time to bond and have fun together. Going on vacation with your father can be a good distraction from the stress of daily life, where you can have fun and enjoy each other's company.

While on vacation, try to leave your problems at home and enjoy your time together. You want to take advantage of this time and seize opportunities to reconnect with your father. The goal is not to have the two of you super serious all the time but rather to have some laughs. During these times, it's important that you ask him how he is doing and make sure that he talks about himself as well. This way, you are able to build a friendship and help get the two of you back on the same page again so that you can rekindle old memories and start over with new ones.

When you decide where you want to go for the vacation, make sure that the place you choose doesn't have any heavy memories attached to it. For example, a vacation to a place where you and your father previously had an argument can remind both of you about the argument. This can make it harder for the two of you to enjoy the vacation because of all the unpleasant memories that are associated with that place. Choosing a new location for your vacation will help keep both of you from having any unpleasant memories from past experiences that may ruin your vacations together.

• **Play Board Games Together**

Board games are one of the most common forms of communication used by children and adults all over the world. Playing board games with your father will help you build a new friendship and allow you both to have fun together. Besides being fun and interesting, board games also help you build your communication skills because for the two of you to either win the game or solve a problem in the game, you must work together and communicate with each other.

By playing board games with your father, you are showing him that there is still hope for the two of you to have fun together and interact in new ways that you haven't done before. This will help you both build trust and communicate with each other again. You are also helping him to feel important and see that he is still needed in your life. This will strengthen your bond with him, so you will better understand each other.

When choosing a board game to play with your father, make sure you choose a game that the two of you can enjoy together. For example, don't choose a super complicated or long game that you both will get bored with because then neither of you will want to finish the game. Also, if your father doesn't really like playing board games, choose a game where he can still participate but doesn't feel as if he is obligated to do so. This way, your father will not get frustrated with the situation and is more likely to have fun with you by playing the game.

- **Organize an Event Together**

When you and your father are able to organize an event together, it can create a new experience for both of you. Instead of doing things at different times, you will organize these activities separately and do them together. The goal is to make an activity that you can enjoy together, not just one where he is forced to do so out of obligation.

When choosing a topic for your event, try to choose something that interests or motivates both of you. For example, if your father likes sports and watching basketball games, then choose a sports-themed event where he gets to watch some basketball games with his friends or even play some basketball himself. This way, you both can have fun while also doing something that you like together.

Organizing this event together shows your father that you are willing to help him in any way you can. Doing so will build trust and communication between the two of you because it shows you are trying to understand what he likes and how he has fun. It also helps build a friendship between the two of you because now, both of you will focus on having a good time rather than arguing or quarreling about what happened in the past. This can create more happiness and joy in your relationship with your father.

• Get Into Good Health Together

Whenever you and your father are able to get into good health, it shows that you are both willing to make a change in your life together. This can help strengthen the bond between the two of you so that it can continue to grow stronger. Getting into good health together shows him that you are willing to change for the better and that you want a positive relationship with him.

When deciding what health-related activity you want, make sure that it is the type of activity you know your father will be interested in participating in. For example, if your father likes running, you should choose a running event since he will be more likely to enjoy something he likes and is used to doing.

This way, you can both have fun while also becoming healthier together.

While getting into good health with your father, it's also important that you both make a real effort because otherwise, this may end up as just another failed attempt at trying to get healthy again. By making a real effort to get healthy, you are showing your father that you are willing to make your relationship a top priority in your life and that you want to work hard with him. This will also help the two of you get closer and build trust with each other.

• Raise a Pet Together

A pet, whether a dog or cat, can be an easy way to bond and communicate with your father. This can help you both to spend more lot time together, closely, emotionally and physically. You can go with you pet for a walk, or you play together in the backyard. These activities these activities implement the development of a serene climate suitable for building bonds, connection and health communication.

When raising a pet, it's important to choose a type of pet your father likes and will enjoy playing with and caring for. For example, if your father is more of the quiet and reserved type, then a dog may not be the best pet for him to have because it will require him to spend more time interacting with it. On the other hand, if your father is more of a person who likes to travel and hang out with friends, then you may choose to get a cat who can still enjoy spending time with you but will also be able to spend some time alone when you are unable to attend to its needs.

When raising a pet together, try not to argue when making decisions so that your father does not feel like you are telling him what he should do. Instead, both of you should discuss what type of pet you are looking to get and then come to an agreement on which one you think would be the best for both of you. Rather than arguing, it will be better to compromise with each other and reach an agreement on which animal is right for you.

• Join an Organization Together

Organizations can be very important in showing your father that you are willing to work with him in an effort to make things better. Joining an organization together shows that you are willing to work towards a common goal so that you and your father can achieve something great together. This can also help you and your father build a positive relationship because you will be forcing yourselves to accomplish something you both want together.

When joining an organization together, you can either choose to join the same organization that your father does or have him join an organization that you are already a member of.

Whichever the choice may be, it is important to choose an organization that your father will be interested in joining so that he will feel more comfortable and motivated to become a part of it. By choosing an organization that he is interested in, it will be easier for him to get involved and make suggestions when it comes to doing things with the group. For example, if your father has a passion for animals, he may benefit from joining a pet-related organization where he can become more involved and help. However, suppose your father is less interested in pets. In such a case, he will not benefit from the group and may become bored, uninterested, and possibly disheartened.

When joining an organization together with your father, make sure that you both take equal responsibility in managing it so that it does not fall apart. Taking equal responsibility for managing the group can help build trust and communication between the two of you because it shows that both of you are committed to looking after it while also being committed to working together. This can be a great way to have fun while also sharing something important together as a family.

• **Repair Something Together**

Sit down with your father when you have time and fix something together. This can be important in showing that you both care about each other, but it's also a great way to bond with your father. Repairing something allows you to get comfortable with each other so that you can work effectively together. It's also a great way to have fun with your father while at the same time strengthening your relationship and understanding of each other.

When repairing something, it's important to make sure you both focus on and enjoy the process. This can be hard when working together because it could mean putting up with each other's faults and problems while being forced to listen to each other talk about things you don't want to hear. However, remembering not to talk about certain things in an effort to avoid your father's faults or problems will help reduce the stress from repairing together. When working together, try not to be too quick with your solutions, either. This will only lead your father to rush and make mistakes that could damage the repaired item, so it's important for you to give him enough time to come up with a solution before offering your own.

Fixing things together can allow you both to express yourselves through physical actions. This can be an effective way to communicate with your father about things you want to discuss, but it's also a good way for both of you to bond on a physical level because you will need to work together as a team.

• Have a Family Dinner Together

Family dinners are an effective way of showing your father that he is important in your life while strengthening your relationship with him on a deep level. By having dinner together every week, it allows both of you to have a moment to talk with each other while enjoying delicious food and conversation. This can be a great way to strengthen your relationship because you will be spending time with your father one-on-one. It's also a great bonding experience for the two of you because you will be forced to work together, cooperate, and talk about important things.

When having dinner together, it's important to take your time with the process itself and not only to get the meal done as quickly as possible. If you try to get everything out of the way and fast, your father will likely be frustrated with the whole thing and may feel that you are not taking his needs seriously. Rather, it's better for you to take your time with things so that you can both enjoy the experience together and communicate with each other in a way that you can both respect and appreciate.

By taking one or more of these actions with your father, you can strengthen your relationship as well as build trust between the two of you. Although it may seem like a large task to accomplish all of these things, it's very important to do so to get the most out of the experience. Being in this kind of relationship with your father is a valuable experience because you can have a great time and help each other out in mutually beneficial and fun ways.

CHAPTER 8: WHEN IT'S TIME TO CUT TIES

U nfortunately, despite the effort you put in while trying to build a close relationship with your father, there are circumstances when you may find that the relationship could be easier to maintain, or it might be dangerous to continue the relationship. In such cases, it's often good to distance yourself from your father, cut him off, and continue an individual healing journey. Such actions are sometimes necessary to prevent further harm to yourself or others.

Situations Where It Is Best to Cut Ties

The following are situations wherein it is usually best to cut ties with your father immediately:

1. Continuous Manipulation and Control

Although you want to be close to him, your father may keep trying to manipulate and control you. This is especially true when your father needs to gain the required skills to express himself clearly and effectively about what he wants you to do for him. When you notice that your father keeps trying to manipulate and control you, it's best that you distance yourself from him to prevent more harm from being done.

It's important for you to distance yourself from someone trying to manipulate and control you because this will protect you from harm. By responding to whatever he says or does, you will grow dependent on him to survive and make him feel powerful over you. This will only worsen things for both of you in the long term, as he will always attempt to manipulate and dominate you to control your life. By allowing him to continue to manipulate and control you, you will become accustomed to his actions, which can cause you to think of yourself as worthless without him.

You may also learn to identify with him as a father and treat others how he treats you, which can cause further problems in your own life. For instance, by learning to manipulate and control others as he did with you, you may become more cold-hearted and cause harm to others to get what you want. On the other hand, if you learn to respond to his manipulation and control by running away or withdrawing from him or others, you may feel alone and helpless.

2. Physical Violence

Although there are many ways in which physical violence manifests itself, all forms of violence are serious and should be taken seriously. By responding to physical violence with physical violence of your own, you will only become trapped in an endless cycle of violence with no hope for escape. An abusive relationship is one where a pattern of behavior causes physical harm or affects a person's sense of self-worth.

This kind of abuse is often considered one of the most severe forms because it is physical. Not only that, but such actions can also cause physical harm, which can have a long-lasting impact on your life and health, as well as psychological harm by leaving emotional scars that never seem to go away no matter how much time passes.

It's often best to distance yourself from your father if you observe him being physically abusive or demonstrating violent tendencies. This is especially true if your father has been physically violent with you in the past, as you will run the risk of him becoming violent towards you again. In addition to breaching the law by physically injuring you or another person, he is likely taking out his troubles and frustrations on you because he feels helpless in other aspects of his life, such as his job or relationships with others.

Many people can tolerate extreme levels of abuse, which is why there are many cases in which a person will continue to be abused by someone known to be abusive. However, continuing such a relationship with your father is not good for you. Such an act will only cause you more harm and worsen the situation by perpetuating the abuse you've already been experiencing without your knowledge. By cutting him out of your life, you will no longer be associated with his abuse or be a victim of it. Rather, you can distance yourself from him and begin your journey toward recovery.

3. Sexual Abuse or Harassment

Sexual harassment is when one person makes unwanted and unwarranted sexual advances towards another person in a way that causes them to feel uncomfortable and threatens their well-being. Sexual assault is when one person forces another to participate in sexual activity against their will through physical contact like kissing, fondling, or penetration with any body part or object.

It's important for you to distance yourself from a father who has been sexually abusive or harassing you and is trying to repeat the same behaviors towards you again. This is because it's likely that he will be continuously trying to repeat the same harmful patterns of behavior to try and get what he wants. If your father continuously tries to make unwanted sexual advances toward you, he likely sees you as an object. This objectification of you is damaging because you'll begin to see yourself as an object to be used or manipulated to meet his needs rather than a human being.

To protect yourself from your father's sexual demands and behavior, you must get away from him immediately. This way, he won't be able to get what he wants by trying to manipulate and control you by making unwanted sexual advances towards you again. You should also report him to the authorities so that he can be stopped from behaving in such a way towards others and that there's no more harm done to you or anyone else.

4. Substance Abuse

Substance abuse is an ongoing pattern of behavior that causes one to physically depend on a drug or other substance, resulting in some behaviors or consequences considered unhealthy or self-destructive, including impaired judgment, poor physical health, and a misplaced sense of self-worth.

If your father is involved in substance abuse in any way, you need to distance yourself from him immediately. This is because substance abuse can become a trap in which you both get stuck in the same cycle of behavior without either of you ever escaping. By staying around him, even if you're trying to help or make things better for him, you will most likely be caught up in the same cycle of behavior that he's already trapped in.

To escape from the trap and break the cycle, you must stop being around him and keep a distance between you. If he continues his substance abuse, he will likely become more dependent on those substances and less dependent on your support or help. Instead of helping him or making things better, you'll just become another person stuck in a pattern of behavior that doesn't allow either of you to grow and change. You also won't be able to help anyone else until you are no longer trapped in such a pattern. By cutting him out of your life, you will free yourself from his control and gain the opportunity to move on with your own life.

5. Gambling Addiction

Gambling addiction is when one person repeatedly bets or plays with money or other items to win to feel some thrill or excitement without actually achieving anything. It can be hard to stop because of its association with risk-taking behavior, which is innate in all humans and, in some cases, a survival instinct. This will cause one to feel an adrenaline rush, thus making them want to continue gambling to experience such feelings again.

Gambling addiction is hard for many people to stop because it is often associated with a loss of control. It's also considered an "impulse control disorder" in which one loses the ability to resist their impulses and has the need for instant gratification of those impulses through the process of gambling. Gambling addicts often manipulate those around them to get money or other things they want but do so in ways that cause others harm or negatively impact their lives. They also are highly likely to experience a great deal of stress during this process because of their continued loss of money and the negative impact on their loved ones.

If your father is involved in this type of behavior, make sure to remove yourself from the situation as soon as possible. If you're not careful, you could get caught up in his behavior and lose control over your own life. Your father may try to manipulate or emotionally blackmail you into helping or giving him money, or he could threaten your life to get you to do what he wants. Any time he does these things to you, it's important for you to distance yourself from him immediately. His behavior will only worsen if you continue your relationship with him.

6. Constant Criticism

There is a limit to criticism, although some people use the word criticism to describe any negative words directed towards the other person. The issue with constant criticism is not how often a person criticizes another but how and why they criticize them. Criticism is actually an expression of one's opinion, whether good or bad, with the intention of providing constructive feedback. Constant criticism is directed at one person throughout an ongoing process to maintain or gain control over them with-out any positive interaction.

If your father is criticizing you constantly, it's best to distance yourself from him as soon as possible. If he continues this be-havior, it will only worsen, and you will feel more isolated and alone. You will begin to lose your sense of self, which can cause a loss of personal identity and purpose. This will also negatively impact your relationships with the people around you because your sense of self is bound to those people in some way, thus may carry you to break off relationships due to the lack of proper care and support.

These situations hurt and damage one's self-esteem, self-worth, and mental health. As you can see, they are all forms of abuse that could cause serious psychological issues if one continues their relationship with those involved in these behaviors. As a result, you need to protect yourself whenever possible and re-move yourself from situations that will only make things worse. Suppose your father is abusing any of these behaviors or even just involved in them in any way. In that case, you need to distance yourself from him immediately, as this will prevent further damage from occurring. When there comes a time when it is necessary for you to part ways with your father, remember that this does not mean you are saying goodbye forever. Recog-nizing when it's time to say goodbye is very difficult because we do not like being separated from someone who has become so important and meaningful in our lives over time. However, that does not mean you shouldn't do it.

First, keep in mind that parting ways is something that cannot be prevented. In fact, ending your relationship with your father is necessary to move forward, build new relationships, and move on with your life. The sooner this happens, the more beneficial it can be for both of you emotionally and mentally. You need to think of your father as a negative force that you need to separate from rather than being angry or sad about saying goodbye to someone who only harmed you. This can help you move on with your life and learn how to open yourself up to new opportunities and relationships.

Parting Ways

When parting ways with your father, several things should be done to make things smoother for everyone involved:

1. Heading It Off Right

In order to lessen the amount of stress and pain your father will be going through when your relationship breaks down, you must prepare yourself by heading off any issues beforehand. This means that you should do everything in your power to try and handle this situation as tactfully as possible without hurting him.

How to do this?

Step 1: Find a Time When You Can Be Alone Together

It's important for you to find a quiet and private place where both of you can talk about this issue calmly and rationally. Only go to this place if there are a few distractions around or if things are happening at the same time. Go somewhere where you can both focus on the conversation at hand, like your bedroom or the living room.

Step 2: Have an Honest Conversation

It's important to have an honest conversation with your father that involves both of you. During this talk, you must tell him everything you feel in your heart and everything you want to say to him. It's important for you to be honest during this talk because this means that you are respecting yourself and your own needs and feelings by being honest with him. So, try to be clear and truthful with what you expect from both of you, hoping it will help ease any tension or stress between you.

For example, you can say, "I've begun to feel like you are trying to control my life, and I'm not comfortable with that. Now that I'm an adult, it's time for me to take ownership of my own life and not be forced into doing things I don't want to do." This will then lead you to how your father's constant criticisms are affecting your self-esteem, which means it's important for him to be honest with himself about the fact that he is only doing this because he doesn't want you to make mistakes.

Step 3: Talk About Your Expectations

As part of the conversation, it's important for you to talk about your expectations and make it clear what it is that you want from them. You should let him know that there are no hard or bad feelings in this situation but that you will end things because this is the best thing for everyone involved. This means that you should lay out how you want things to go down between you and him afterward and what he should expect from you in saying goodbye to each other now. This will help both of you to understand the other's perspective and make a choice based on what's best for both of you, as opposed to one of you pursuing change and the other resisting it.

For example, you can say, "I'm going to try and keep in touch with you, but I may not be as available. I'm sure I'll be busy at times, and the same goes for you, so it'll be hard to have a relationship as we used to." This will show that you're upfront about your intentions and not trying to avoid this issue. Instead, you're trying to make it easy for him so he is not surprised about your decision to end things.

Step 4: Be Clear About Your Decision

This is the moment when you will have to tell your father that it's time for you to say goodbye. So, take a deep breath and then say something like, "I know you love me, and I love you, too, but there comes a time when our lives have changed so much that it's inevitable for us to part ways with each other." Try to be as clear as possible about the fact that this isn't anyone's fault and that sometimes relationships end because life happens. Then say something like, "We've been through a lot together and had many happy times, but things have changed between us, and I'm not sure if we can ever return to how they were before." Then, you should end the conversation by saying something like, "I know it's hard for you to hear this, but I want you to know that I'm thinking about moving on with my life, and it's best for us if you do the same. And please don't be mad at me or upset because I never wanted this to happen in the first place. Instead, know that I love you and that this has nothing to do with how much I care about you. And even though our relationship is ending now, there is no need for either of us to feel sad about this."

This will offer you more time to move on with your life without your father's assistance, and it will also demonstrate that you are not angry with him and that this is beyond his control. And if he wants to reach out to you after everything has been said, he can do so as long as he pleases. But, in the end, you'll both understand why things were like this in the first place, and being able to move on with your life in a healthy way will help you get through all of this much easier.

2. Set Clear Boundaries

Even though it's important for you to talk to your father about this and prepare yourself for the hardest part, that doesn't mean you should wait to set clear boundaries. Instead, setting them up as soon as possible will make things much easier for both of you in the long run.

How do you do this?

Step 1: Make a List of Your Boundaries

When making a list of your boundaries, think about how you want to keep things between you and your father. So, think about what's important for you and make a list of as many of these things as possible. Then, make another list that includes the boundaries that you will set to prevent future problems.

For example, if one is important to you, it might be saying that he shouldn't criticize or be judgmental towards others during conversations with you; another might be setting clear guidelines for when he should have private time with you, and so on. As long as you keep these boundaries in writing, it will be easy to show him and discuss them if there are any problems with how he is treating you.

Step 2: Set Up a Time to Talk About This

After making a list, schedule time with your father to talk about this in person. The best course of action is to meet during the day and ensure that both of you are in a good mood and feeling good about yourselves prior to having this conversation so that he is more receptive. The worst time is at night or when things have been going wrong for either of you, so keep this in mind before making a choice.

Step 3: Talk About Your Boundaries and Expectations

Make sure to use the list as a guide for everything that needs to be said, and avoid using words like **"always."** Instead, use words like, **"this will likely happen"** or **"this is important."** When discussing boundaries, ensure you're being clear, honest, fair, and truthful. If your father does not agree with your boundaries and expectations once they are clearly stated, you might have to have a second talk after making some time for both of you to cool down and think about everything.

Step 4: Give Your Father a Chance to Respond

When having this conversation, make sure to give your father plenty of time to respond with honest words. You should be as open as possible and clear that you're making these boundaries because it is best for both of you. If he asks why, you should say, **"I think it's better for us if we do things this way**

because it will prevent more problems in the future." If you go around and around about everything, you might have to schedule another conversation to meet in person.

Once he understands your needs, your father will know that there is nothing he can do that will change the way things are going between you. The hard part will be deciding not to react personally and instead listening with an open mind so he can hear what you are saying. When this happens, you should be sure to leave the room or any place where you have this talk so your father doesn't feel like he has to defend himself. This is why it's best if both of you have private time during which he can listen and understand without feeling defensive or sentimental.

Step 5: Be Prepared to Follow Through

Once you have set clear boundaries and expectations, know that you will have to stick to them. If your father does not respect and see the importance of these boundaries, then it'll be up to you to call a time out and end all contact with that person for a time until things get better. If you don't do this, then you might feel stuck with someone who does not listen to your needs and wants.

In the end, it will be important for you to follow through with whatever happens in your relationship to find peace of mind and ensure that nothing like this happens again in the future. So, if things get better or worse, then know that you are prepared for everything and that there is no room for doubt because of the steps taken to understand what's going on between the two of you now.

When parting ways with your father, boundaries and expectations will be the most important things for you to set; by setting them up, even if your father does not understand why, you will feel more confident about moving forward healthily. And, when you feel this way, you'll know nothing else can be done other than moving forward.

Step by step, you'll find your way to a place where you feel comfortable letting go of the angry feelings that have been pulling at your heart without allowing them to completely take over. That's why you should make this process as clear as possible and know that the steps taken are going to matter so much more than anything that your father says.

The emotionally absent father is something that we have all experienced, whether through our real fathers or our stepfathers, or even friends who have been distant during tough times in our lives. These people are not bad people; they are just struggling with their own issues and need help dealing with them before they can see beyond their own pain. In the end, they always have a choice whether they will be present in our lives or not. Even when they do make that choice and decide to come back into our lives, we must remember that it is up to us whether we will let them back into our lives. As long as you know how these relationships affect you, you won't find yourself struggling and can start to heal the pain that the past has caused so that you can move forward in peace and enjoy your life today.

Knowing when and how to cut ties with your father is important. It is also important to understand why you want to cut ties and what will happen as a result of your decisions. It is not always easy to make the right choice, but it will be worth it in the long run, especially when you see the change that happens when you do.

PART 4: HEALING EMOTIONAL WOUNDS: RECOVERING SELF-ESTEEM AND CONFIDENCE

CHAPTER 9: BECOME AWARE OF YOUR PAIN

A cknowledging the pain you feel is part of the healing process. When you allow yourself to be honest about your hurt and fear, you can begin to understand it better and figure out how to manage it. It is also important that every pain you are feeling is not only your emotionally absent father's fault. It is just the by-product of being hurt and wanting love from a specific person who is, unfortunately, unable to give love.

Ways to Become Aware of Your Pain

The following are some of the techniques you can use to be aware of your emotions:

1. Mindfulness

Maintaining kind and compassionate awareness of your thoughts, emotions, physical sensations, and external environment is what mindfulness entails. Acceptance is also a part of mindfulness, which means that you will pay attention to your thoughts and feelings without judging them. When you practice mindfulness, you will not think about the past or the future. Instead, you will think about what you're feeling right now. In the present moment, you will become fully aware of your feelings and thoughts.

Several Exercises to Practice Mindfulness:

a. Body Scan Meditation

The body scan is a type of mindfulness meditation in which you look over your body for pain, tension, or anything else that seems out of place. It can help you feel more in touch with your body and your emotions.

How to do this?

Step 1: Get Comfortable

Lay down or sit in a way that makes stretching your arms and legs easy.

Step 2: Focus on Your Breathing

Then close your eyes and pay attention to how you're breathing. Deeply inhale through the nose before exhaling through the mouth. You can begin at your head, your left foot, your right hand, or your right foot. Keep looking at that spot and take slow, deep breaths. Then do the same thing with another part of your body.

Step 3: Pay Attention

Open your mind to pain, tension, discomfort, or anything else that feels different. Spend 20 seconds to a minute paying attention to these feelings. If you start to feel pain or discomfort, notice it and sit with any feelings it brings. Don't say anything bad about them. For example, don't criticize yourself for feeling frustrated and angry. Pay attention to them and let them go. Keep breathing and imagine the pain and stress going away with each breath.

Step 4: Release

Slowly take your mind off that part of your body and move it to the next thing you want to focus on. Some people find it helpful to imagine letting go of one part of their body as they breathe out and the next as they breathe in. Continue the exercise along your body in a way that makes sense to you, either from top to bottom or from one side to the other. Pay attention to when your thoughts wander as you keep scanning your body. Don't worry; this is likely to happen more than once. You have succeeded, and getting back on the right track is easy. Slowly bring your attention back to where you were when you stopped scanning.

Step 5: Visualize and Breathe

Once you're done looking at different parts of your body, let your awareness move over your whole body. Imagine a mold being filled with liquid. Continue to slowly breathe in and out as you sit there for a few seconds with this awareness of your whole body. Take note of how your body feels and what you're thinking. Try to be with your body and notice what's going on without trying to change or judge anything.

Step 6: Release

Release any tension, pain, or discomfort with a deep breath. Then open your eyes and gently stretch out your body.

b. Sitting Meditation

Similar to body scans, sitting meditation is also a mindfulness practice where you pay attention to the present moment and what you are thinking, feeling, or sensing. The only difference is that you sit while practicing it.

How to do this?

Step 1: Find a Comfortable Sitting Position

Sit in a way that keeps your spine straight and makes it easy for you to breathe. You can also sit on a pillow or folded yoga mat if your back is too sore from sitting comfortably on the floor. If sitting up feels awkward for you at first, you can start by lying down with your eyes closed. Once you're comfortable with that, try sitting up and looking at a spot on the wall or the ground. If you want to look at something in particular, try drawing a circle on the ground with your finger.

Step 2: Breathe and Feel

Try to relax and focus on your breath. It's okay if you feel your heart beating for a moment. Find a way to notice how it makes you feel or where it is in your body. Slowly inhale through your nose and keep breathing as long as you need to get used to breathing slowly. When you're ready, use the exhale to let go of any feelings or thoughts that are bothering you. You can also focus on relaxing each part of your body as you breathe out.

Step 3: Stay With Your Breath

As thoughts enter your mind, bring your attention back to your breath. Don't judge yourself for thinking about anything, and don't try to get rid of your thoughts. Just notice them and return your awareness to how you're breathing. Keep doing this until you can stay with the flow of your breath without letting any other thoughts or feelings interrupt it. It's a good idea not to spend more than 10 minutes on this practice in one session. When you need a break from sitting, get up and do something else for a few minutes before sitting down again.

Step 4: Release and Rest

When your practice is done, do a few gentle stretches. Then sit for several minutes with your eyes closed and admire what you've learned about yourself. If you need to, do some more mindful breathing until you feel calm and relaxed. When your mind starts to wander, gently notice that it is thinking rather than trying to get rid of the thoughts or doing anything else until they go away. If it feels helpful, you can think of something positive or aspire toward something you want to refocus your attention on the present moment.

c. Walking Meditation

This is a simple form of meditation where you focus on walking meditation as you go about your day. The basic idea behind it is that if you're constantly worrying or ruminating over what happened in the past, there's no room for anything new in your mind. By focusing on things right in front of you, however, you can find room in your thoughts for new possibilities.

How to do this?

Step 1: Find a Quiet Place

Find a place where you have plenty of room to walk away from sounds like phones, traffic, or people that you don't want to hear.

Step 2: Pay Attention and Feel

Take a few deep breaths and start walking at a pace that feels good for you while focusing on different parts of your body. Notice how each step feels as it happens, how much weight is on the bottom of each foot, and how it feels to move through space with each step. Take note of any physical sensations in your body worth noticing. Then let these sensations go after they pass by without giving them much importance in your life.

Step 3: Stay With Your Body

Rather than thinking about what's going on in your life, try to be with your body. Focus on noticing how it moves from when you start walking. Don't judge yourself for not getting things done, and don't try to get your mind off those worries that are getting in the way. It's fine if you have thoughts about what might go wrong or wonder if you've forgotten something important, but that doesn't mean it's urgent or that you're bound to remember it. When you realize your mind has wandered, gently bring it back to your walk and let any other thoughts go.

Step 4: Notice the Good

See what you can notice that makes you feel good. Try to appreciate your body and the space around you. Appreciate that you're alive and can enjoy moving throughout your day. Give yourself credit for doing something different, even if it seems insignificant or small. Focus on how good you'll feel when your meditation is finished or how nice it will be when it's over.

Mindfulness can help you identify the pain and suffering you're experiencing and let go of it. The purpose of each practice is to develop an awareness of what is occurring in the present moment without allowing the mind to wander into the past or future. Doing so allows you to think about what you want or need to do in the present moment.

2. Writing Things Down

Writing is like meditating but keeps your brain busy. This is because writing forces you to focus and get clear about your thoughts and feelings. Whenever you find yourself feeling overwhelmed, instead of suppressing your feelings, writing down what is bothering you can help you understand it better. It can help you be more rational and calm down.

Below is an activity where you can write down your thoughts and feelings:

a. Journaling

Journaling is a way to express yourself without being judged. You don't have to show your journal to anyone else or tell people what you're writing about. This can make it easier to be more honest and open in your writing. It is also a way to keep track of your thoughts and emotions throughout the day. When you read over what you wrote, there are patterns among your thoughts and feelings that can give clues about what you're going through.

How to do this?

Step 1: Ready Your Materials

To begin, all you need is a pen and a journal or notebook of any sort. It can be enjoyable to select your preferred pen and an inspiring journal. You can get a variety of journals, pencils, markers, stickers, and other embellishments for your journal by searching online or visiting any book, stationary, or office supply retailer. The more varied your journaling materials are, the more pleasurable it will be to write in them.

Step 2: Find a Quiet Space

Find a place to relax and reflect on the subject you wish to write about. You can sit or stand comfortably, but ensure you are fully awake and alert. Remove any distractions such as ringing phones, your TV, or your computer. This doesn't mean you need to isolate yourself from the rest of the world or close all the doors in your room; it just means spending time on yourself without other people's voices and noises distracting you. This can be done at home, in your bedroom, or wherever else you feel comfortable.

Step 3: Get Calmer First

Before writing anything down, take a moment to notice how you feel right now. Write down how you feel in a few sentences or draw a picture. You can also think about what you've been doing today and when you started feeling this way. This is all information that should be included in your entry.

Step 4: Write Down Your Thoughts and Feelings

When you are ready to begin writing, open up your journal and write whatever comes to mind. Let yourself feel whatever emotion you're feeling when you're writing it down. You can also write about what happened that day or what you need to do as soon as possible. Don't try to figure out what this means for the future or what other people think about it; just let it go and write about how it affects you. If you have difficulty concentrating, write down whatever comes into your head without trying to make sense of it, analyze it, or get anything else done. This is about getting everything on your mind down on paper.

For example:

- *"I'm feeling _____ (what you are feeling at the moment) because _____ (write down what you are thinking and why you are feeling that way)."*

- *"Today, I wrote in my journal. The day started off well, but then it wasn't so good when _____ (write down what you were doing and what happened when you were feeling this way). After doing _____ (what you did), I was feeling _____ (write down how you felt after doing it) because _____ (what happened). It's really hard for me to think about those things again and again, and the more I think about them, the more it hurts."*

As long as your writing is clear and concise, you can write as much or as little as you like. Don't worry about how long it will take to write the entry or if you will ever finish it. Don't try to figure out what this entry means for your future.

Step 5: Reflect on What You've Written

When you finish putting down everything on paper, reflect on what you have written. Review your writing and think about how it makes you feel. If you feel sad, let yourself cry, and then write down how you feel after crying. Write about why you are sad or what makes you cry. Alternatively, if you're angry, write down how angry you feel and try to explain why that anger is there. Sometimes the reason we get upset may only be readily apparent once the situation has settled a bit. Then when it is clear, we can articulate why we were so angry in the first place.

Step 6: Look Over What You've Written

Once you have finished reflecting on what you have written, go back and look over what you wrote. If you are still thinking about the entries from earlier, which may be much of the time when you're writing a journal entry, read them aloud. Doing so may cheer you up and help you remember what happened earlier in your life. Reviewing your writing may also provide insight into how to solve your current problem or heal your emotions.

In this way, writing can help us understand our emotions better so that we can use our emotions as guidance for changes we want to make in our life instead of our emotions controlling us from within.

How long should I do this?

It is up to you how long you should keep a journal. Writing in a journal can be fun and helpful, so make sure you understand why or what you're doing before committing yourself to this activity. You can keep a journal as little or as long as you want; it's flexible. Just remember that if writing in a journal helps you with your life, it should be done every day, even if it's just one page.

Journaling is beneficial because it enables you to express yourself in ways that are not always possible through conversation. In a journal, you always say what's important to you, no matter who else is listening or reading. This can be very beneficial as it allows you to become aware of the pain that may be underneath what you're saying.

3. Get Honest Feedback From Others

Often, others have a better perspective on us than we do, especially our closest friends and relatives. These people know us better than we know ourselves and can see things about us that we may not even be able to see. The pain and trauma that a person may feel can be starker to them than it could to anyone else, and they may be able to see things that are hidden from others. This can provide valuable insight into how your current situation might appear to others and give you some perspective on your own life.

How to do this?

Step 1: Select Your Close Friends and Relatives

The people that you choose should be the ones who will give you honest feedback without judgment or bias. It's important that these people know what has happened in your life, how it has affected your emotions, and how it has impacted you today. The people who may be best for this job are close family members or friends who really understand you and are just there for you. It's important that these people know what is important to you and that you can trust them enough to tell them.

Step 2: Talk About the Issue

When you talk to these people, be honest with them and take your time to explain everything you can remember. It's important that they can see the situation clearly, so they know what they are talking about while they give you honest feedback. Don't be too hard on yourself; it's normal for people to not fully understand what happened when something traumatic occurs, especially if it happened years ago. During this part of the process, be sure to ask these individuals questions to explain things more fully and clarify things that might not have been clear in your memory.

Questions like:

- "What do you think about what I told you?"

- "What do you think about when I say
  _____ (something that
  happened that hurt you or is a source of pain in your
  life)"

- "I'm confused about why
  _____ (insert something that
  happened). Can you help me figure out why this happened?"

It is very helpful to ask these individuals which of their answers gives you more information on the issue and if they have a solution for your current situation. Remember, it's not their responsibility to solve your problems for you; they are just there to give their honest feedback, free from judgments and biases. They are not looking to control what you do or cause you to change; they want you to see yourself through their eyes to understand what is happening better.

Step 3: Understand Their Explanations

After listening to your feedback, understand how it makes sense to them. Try and think about what they're saying and why they may be giving certain explanations. This can help clarify things in your head and allow you to understand the problem in your life more clearly. In this way, more light will come on the issue, allowing you to know how the situation impacted your emotions at that time and how it's affecting you today if it's still a source of pain and trauma.

Step 4: Think About What You're Going to Do Next

After you think things over, care about the situation, and understand what it is and how it's affecting you today, you should be able to make some decisions on how to handle the issue in your life. You'll better understand what happened in your life and your options for dealing with the problems from that point in your life. This will help you know where you're going next so that you can move forward with your life, heal yourself, and find a solution to the problem to start moving on from this part of your life.

Sometimes, when you're done talking to these people, you may need clarification about the issue, which can cause you to doubt the decisions you want to make. In this case, talking with a counselor or professional might help you think things over more fully and decide what will be best for your situation. It's also important that these people understand that some things may not be as clear as others, and there may not always be an answer for everything. This is normal, especially when there are some things we can't remember that may be hidden in our subconscious; however, having people trained to help with these kinds of problems can be helpful.

Discussing difficult topics can be very uncomfortable for many people. However, understanding what happened to you and how your emotions are affected by the events will help you gain insight into how to move on from this problem and what kind of life you want for yourself going forward. It can also help you understand that there are times when things happen that we cannot control, and we must learn how to let those events go so we can move on from them.

CHAPTER 10: EXERCISES AND STRATEGIES TO OVERCOME INSECURITY AND LACK OF SELF-ESTEEM

I nsecurity and the lack of self-esteem are one of the biggest effects that your emotionally absent father has had on your life. One way these issues have affected you is that you feel as if you don't have the power to change anything about the situation; you feel powerless and cannot make any improvements in your life.

By overcoming your insecurities and boosting your self-esteem, you can advance in life and attain the level of happiness you deserve.

The following are the exercises that are designed to help you overcome the insecurity and lack of self-esteem that your emotionally absent father has had on your life:

1. Improve Yourself Physically

To boost your confidence and improve your self-esteem, you should always strive to improve yourself physically. Although some women don't always like to admit it, looking good is a great way to boost your confidence in yourself and increase self-esteem. How you look is often a reflection of what you feel about yourself; therefore, when you feel good about yourself, you will always try to look good.

How to do this?

There are numerous ways to improve your physical condition:

a. Regular Exercise

It has been shown that women who exercise regularly have a significantly lower risk of heart disease, and they are also at a lower risk of depression. By working out and staying fit, you will find that your confidence will shoot up, and you will feel better about yourself. In addition to boosting your confidence and self-esteem, it will also improve your mood and make you feel more at ease. Being more relaxed helps you overcome the stress in your life and makes it simpler to be happy and calm.

Simple Exercises That Boost Your Confidence and Body

I. Walking

Walking is low-impact, does not require much space or equipment, and can be performed anywhere. You can walk around your neighborhood, go out to the park, or even walk outside.

It is recommended that you walk for at least 30 minutes every day. This helps to build your strength, get fit, and increase your endurance, which helps you handle stress better, and it will give you more energy to deal with problems in life at a quicker pace because you won't be tired from being tired when you finish exercising. If you want to push yourself even further, you can also walk longer distances outside. You can also do this when traveling or commuting to work; through this, you will strengthen your cardiovascular system and get fit while on the go.

ii. Running/Jogging

Another low-impact exercise that is great for boosting your confidence is running and jogging. While walking is a low-impact exercise, running gives you a higher-intensity workout, as it puts more stress on your body. This means that running helps relieve stress, gives you a higher rate of fat burning, and helps strengthen your muscles.

It is recommended that you take a day when you can go running or jog outside and walk to get the most out of your run. It is also recommended that you run for at least 3 miles at a time at a level of intensity that you are comfortable with. It is also recommended that you try jogging for 5 miles daily. It is also important that you wear the proper shoes while exercising so that they are comfortable on your feet. You don't want to be distracted by foot pain or shoes that are too tight and uncomfortable.

iii. Biking

Another great form of exercise is biking; almost everyone knows how to ride a bike, which makes it easily accessible. Biking is also a simple exercise that can be done indoors, outdoors, and even on the road for commuting to work. Riding a bike is also great because it helps strengthen your leg muscles and increase your endurance. This means that biking is great for improving your overall fitness level, building muscle mass, and increasing lean muscle mass, which will help boost your confidence.

You can always try to get a bike that helps you get a workout. Different bikes with different settings will also make your cycle more enjoyable and fun. It is also recommended that you bike anywhere between 20 minutes to 30 minutes every day, depending on your physical fitness level, to get the best from your bike. It is important that you also wear comfortable clothing when you ride your bike. A bag basket, a sun visor for additional comfort and sun protection, and lights for safety in case it gets dark where you are riding are all fun additions that can make your bike more enjoyable.

iv. Swimming

Swimming is another excellent form of exercise; it is a fantastic way to stay fit and improve your health. When you are in the water, you will find that your body weight is fully supported, which means that this exercise is very low-impact. This way, you can swim without worrying about straining your joints or injuring yourself. Swimming is also considered to be one of the most effective full-body workouts since it works on all of the muscles in your body. This means that swimming is very effective in burning a lot of calories as well as improving your physical fitness level and overall health tremendously.

It is recommended that you swim for at least 30 minutes every day. It is also important that you try to swim with friends or at a pool with lanes so that you can set a goal for yourself and your friends to keep pushing each other and encourage one another to go the distance. You can also do other things like swimming laps, swimming in the deep end, or even trying some lightweight training in the water and see how effective it is.

v. Yoga/Pilates/Aerobics

Another great form of exercise that is recommended is one where you focus on building up your core muscles. This helps you strengthen your body and makes it more flexible. This type of exercise will also improve your posture, which will boost your confidence by making you look more beautiful and attractive. Not only that, when you are in a yoga or Pilates class, it can be an excellent way to meet new friends and socialize while also getting fit.

It is recommended to find a professional to teach you the basics, as well as special techniques. This way, you will know how to do these exercises correctly and effectively so you can stay safe at the same time. It is important that you take a class at least 3 times a week, and you can choose from a variety of classes including, but not limited to, yoga, Pilates, aerobics, and more. You can also try doing other types of exercises, such as weight training and push-ups, by practicing on your own.

Sometimes, it takes a lot of time and effort to get the desired results; in this case, it's important not to get discouraged and continue trying your best. As long as there is an effort to improve yourself physically, that's one step forward that gets you closer and closer to improving your self-esteem.

b. Eat Healthily

Eating healthy is another great way to improve your physical appearance and the quality of your life and make you feel better overall; therefore, it will help improve your self-esteem.

Tips on Eating Healthy

a. Eat Fresh Fruits and Vegetables

Eating plenty of vegetables is a great way to add more nutrients to your diet, making you feel healthier and improving your skin's condition. Fresh fruits, such as watermelon, raspberries, strawberries, grapefruits, peaches, cantaloupes, and oranges, are abundant in antioxidants that protect the skin from the sun's damaging rays. Vegetables like broccoli, broccoli sprouts, cauliflower, and zucchini are very low in calories and sugar, so they will not only help you lose weight but also keep you feeling full all the time as well as satisfied.

It is recommended that you eat 2 to 3 servings of fresh fruits and vegetables every day. If you are going to buy them, choose the ones that are fresh, not frozen or canned. The best time to eat these foods is first thing in the morning when your stomach is empty. Eating them this way will give your body a boost of nutrients that it needs. Also, try to drink plenty of water after eating your veggies because they help flush out all the toxins in your body and boost energy levels in your body. When you feel healthier and happier about yourself, it will reflect on how much more confident you are, as well.

ii. Eat Whole Grains

Another great thing that you can do is eat whole grains; their benefits are many when it comes to improving your physical health and making you feel better overall. Whole grains like wheat, oatmeal, brown rice, or quinoa are great source of complex carbohydrates, which is important in supplying the energy your body needs to release stored fats into the bloodstream. Whole grains are also high in protein, which means that the amount of protein in your diet will help improve your muscle condition. Whole grains also come with many other vitamins and minerals that will balance out other nutrients in your body and give you a boost of energy to keep you going throughout the day.

Eating at least 4 to 6 servings of whole grains a day is recommended, but you can choose between white rice, brown rice, quinoa, and other alternatives like buckwheat. It is important that you try to eat smaller portions of whole grains as compared with other foods. If you are still looking for whole grains at your local market, buying them online is recommended because they are a lot cheaper than buying the same grain at the grocery store. Before eating your grains, or any other food for that matter, try to rinse them off so that they don't have any extra added calories and unhealthy fats in the food.

iii. Eat Protein

Eating plenty of protein is also an essential part of your diet because it helps you feel stronger and healthier overall. Protein can be found in a variety of sources like fish, seafood, eggs, lean meats, and poultry. Some people tend to shy away from eating lean meats and other protein forms because they believe they are fattening or unhealthy; however, this is far from true. When you eat lean meats and other types of protein, it helps to keep your body strong and healthy while also preventing illness and disease.

Eating at least 3 servings of protein every day is recommended, but if you want to lose weight, limit your intake. If you are going to eat protein at a meal, it is important that you eat them with whole grains and fresh fruits or vegetables because they help with digestion and add the extra nutritional value that your body needs. The best time to eat all types of protein is at breakfast because it will give you an energy boost as well as keep you full until lunchtime. You don't need to be obsessed with the quantity of protein in your body; control and moderation is the key.

iv. Avoid Junk Food and Processed Meals

Junk foods, such as candy bars, potato chips, and french fries, are generally unhealthy for many different reasons, such as being high in sodium, fat, carbohydrates, and refined grains that are not recommended for consumption at all. Processed food is very processed and often contains chemicals that can cause health problems such as cancer or other types of diseases in individuals when consumed on a regular basis. When you consume junk food and processed meals, it is not only bad for your body but also bad for your mentality. It makes you feel sluggish, tired, and less energized, making you feel like you can't do anything in your life, ultimately impacting your confidence level and self-esteem.

It is recommended that you avoid these foods because they are completely unhealthy; if you are addicted to them, try to reduce your consumption by at least 50 percent. Try substituting some of these foods with food options that are healthier for your body and will not leave you completely drained.

You can do many things to eat healthy, nutritious, and delicious foods without feeling like you're missing out on your favorite unhealthful foods. By doing so, you will be happier and healthier and feel better about yourself as well.

c. Looking Better

There are ways to make yourself look better that don't necessarily involve you having to change how you eat or how much you sleep. Simply making sure that you're wearing good clothing, getting your hair cut, and taking care of your skin will also greatly impact how you feel about yourself and how you project your image to others.

Tips for Looking Good

i. Wear Clothing That Makes You Feel Good

There is different clothing that makes you feel good, and wearing them will also make you look good. For example, a lot of people choose to wear comfortable clothes that reflect their personalities but also make them look good in the process. Some people wear hoodies, sweatpants, and other comfortable clothing that they feel is more casual but very fashionable; however, many also choose to wear clothing that feels both fashionable and comfortable. Some people like to have their own fashion style, which is different from the majority of other people in the fashion industry.

The best way to make yourself look good is by wearing fashionable and comfortable clothes. If you do this, you will look better because you will be adding a certain style that would otherwise not be there while wearing them. You will also feel better because it's important to feel comfortable while at work or out with your friends and family.

ii. Pay Attention to Your Hair and Skin

You can also pay attention to some of the other parts of your body by making sure that they are kept clean and healthy through daily bathing and moisturizing. Bathing and moisturizing are easy ways to keep yourself looking good because they will also keep your skin and hair healthy. You must also maintain a regular cleansing routine for your hair, which may include shampooing, rinsing, and conditioning.

Makeup is another way that you can enhance certain features of your face or body that may be less than attractive such as dark circles under your eyes or blemishes so you feel better about yourself. If you do not like wearing makeup but want to look better and feel better about how you appear in public, try using a tinted moisturizer or foundation for a more natural look. This will also help your skin look healthier.

Doing these things will enhance your appearance in public, which will make you feel better and more comfortable in your own skin. This will also make you feel happier because you will love yourself more than before.

The way you see yourself physically can greatly affect your self-esteem and happiness, so it's important that you are always confident and happy with who you are. This can be done by making small changes to your everyday life that can help you feel better about yourself. By making a few changes to the way you eat and act every day, you will ultimately feel better and see yourself differently.

2. Experiment With Creative Expression

Finding a way to express yourself creatively can be helpful to relax and release emotional tension because it will make you feel better about yourself and feel like you are in more control of your life. Feeling more in control of yourself gives you the confidence and self-esteem to go out and make changes to your life so that you can have a better life and improve your quality of life.

The following are some creative expressions that you can use to improve your self-esteem and confidence:

a. Music

Singing, dancing, playing an instrument, or even listening to music can be a good way to express yourself. Expressing yourself through music is a great way to let go of your feelings and focus on the physical sounds that you are making; it's a more active approach to creative expression. This can be helpful for people who are going through tough times and need some release from what they are going through because it will make them feel better about themselves in the long run.

You do not need any instruments or skills to make your voice heard. If you enjoy singing, go ahead and sing; it is a great way to express how you feel about yourself. It does not matter if you are not the greatest singer or don't like to sing in front of other people. It can be done while you are alone in your car or while sitting quietly at home late at night. If you like dancing, get out there and dance; you can dance in your bedroom or move around the house without anyone seeing you. It doesn't matter if you've never danced before because you'll pick up the rhythm and steps as you go. You can dance as slow or fast as you want without worrying about being judged.

Music can help express emotions, feelings, and thoughts that many people have but do not always know how to express themselves. It can also improve your self-esteem by making you let go of your daily problems and think of something else for a while.

b. Art

Many people who have been inspired by art say that it helps them to get in the zone and create without thinking about what they are doing or making. Art is all around you and can be done in a variety of ways, including painting, drawing, creating crafts, and even sculpting. Whatever your artistic preference, painting is a great way to let off some steam by creating something with no restrictions on how you want it to look; it's all up to you and how you want to create it.

Only you can explain exactly what you are creating. This will also allow you to think of nothing but the painting and what you are going to do next. This can have an effect on your mind by relieving tension and stress, which will make you feel better about yourself in the long run.

You do not have to be a professional artist or draw something that looks like it came from the hand of an expert. You can draw your own interpretation of a face, a dog, or whatever you feel like drawing. It depends on how you wish to express yourself. You also only need a little material to start with; you can use a pencil, crayon, marker, or paint by using your imagination and seeing where it takes you. It's a great way to kill time when you're feeling stressed and need to think about something other than what's going on around you.

c. Writing

Writing has also been a way for many people to express themselves in times of stress or emotional pain; it's a good alternative to talking when you don't know what to say or how to say it. Whether it's a journal, short stories, poetry, or anything else you can think of that you can write down, it's a good creative outlet to help keep you from breaking down and getting overwhelmed. This will help you express what you are feeling, which will help you feel better about yourself.

Something about the written word can be a powerful way for people to express themselves. If you want to write stories, take a trip down memory lane or write down your thoughts when it comes to life and love. If you want to write poems and short stories, it's all up to you and how creative and free of restrictions you want your writing to be. You can even combine different creative expressions into one piece if that interests you; it's all up to your creativity and imagination.

As long as you express yourself through your creative outlets, it will help you feel better. Don't worry if you are not the most creative person in the world; everyone is different, and everyone has their own interpretation of what they think is creative. Just go with whatever your interpretation of creativity is; so long as you are doing something that will release the tension in your mind and calm you down, then that's all that matters.

3. Practice Self-Compassion

Many daughters of emotionally absent fathers have developed a sense of self-blame and self-judgment, so practicing self-compassion can be a useful exercise to help overcome these negative emotions and feelings.

The following are some ways that you can do in order to practice self-compassion:

a. Affirming Oneself With Kindness

Words have a powerful impact on all aspects of human health, from physical to mental to emotional stability. Words are energies that carry sounds and meanings, and the combination of these two elements can be harnessed for good or bad. To help overcome self-blame, try using positive affirmations to boost your self-confidence and counter negative feelings about yourself.

Self-affirmations are positive words that you tell yourself in order to encourage healing and understand your own worth. Affirmations are usually thoughts that are repeated over and over. The repetition helps solidify the positive belief in your subconscious mind, which will allow you to change your belief systems.

For instance, if your father was emotionally unavailable and you have developed negative self-beliefs and self-blame, it may be beneficial to repeat the following affirmations:

"I am loved. Others care about me."

"I am able to overcome any obstacles."

"I am a good person and have positive qualities."

"I can trust others to support me in times of need."

"I am deserving of love."

"I am worthy of my own happiness."

"I am strong, and my life is worthwhile."

"I have a purpose of living on."

The repetition of these words will begin to change your belief about yourself and your worth. The more you repeat the affirmation, the more it will become a reality for you. It is helpful to start with small things, such as repeating affirmations on a daily basis.

b. Acknowledge Your Qualities And Merits

One way that you can practice self-compassion is by acknowledging your qualities and merits and recognizing your strengths. This will help you become more self-aware of your capabilities and weaknesses, allowing you to overcome them.

The other way you can practice self-compassion is by acknowledging your weakness and admit that you tend to make mistakes or do things wrong from time to time. This will allow you to be more aware of the fact that you are human and that no matter how well-prepared you are, there will always be things about yourself that can make or break the situation.

How to do this?

Step 1: Write All Your Qualities and Merits

The first step is to list all of your qualities and accomplishments. This includes your strengths, personality traits, or skills you have mastered, such as courage, creativity, etc. If it is too challenging to write it all down in a single sitting, then you can take it at a gradual pace by writing down a few things at a time and continue writing longer as you go along.

For example, you can write down things like intelligence, kindness, bravery, compassion, and many more. You can also include your qualities, such as love and generosity. You can take it back and review them as you feel the need to do so. They will help inspire you to become better by challenging yourself to be the best you can be.

Step 2: Identify Your Negatives and Weaknesses

The second step is to identify your negatives and weaknesses to learn from and work on them. Acknowledge that there are many things about yourself that are not perfect or flawless. This will give you the motivation to continue improving yourself so that you may eventually no longer have any of these negative attributes in your life.

Reflect on your weaknesses and acknowledge that they are not the end of the world. Consider what needs to be done to improve and correct them. For example, if you feel you need more confidence with public speaking, take it upon yourself to practice speaking in front of others when necessary. To build on your strengths, you can also work on improving your weaknesses by having a goal for what you want to improve. You can set up this goal through an exercise like setting a challenge or drawing up plans for improving yourself. This will help you determine what you ultimately want and how to achieve it.

Step 3: Practice Gratitude

The last step is to practice humility because this is the best way for you to appreciate yourself and learn from your mistakes. Instead of telling yourself that you are not good enough, acknowledge that everyone can make mistakes and can work on improving themselves for the better. Instead of saying negative things about yourself, be grateful that you have so many positive qualities, which will give you the motivation to become a better person and realize your potential.

By acknowledging your talents and skills, you can learn from your weaknesses and work on them. By practicing gratitude, you will also be able to appreciate yourself and see the value that you bring to the world. You will also learn that no matter how strong you believe you are, there are some things beyond your control and that sometimes, what is in your heart is more important than what is in your hands.

By having self-compassion, your self-esteem will increase, affecting your relationships and interactions with others in your life. You will be able to accept what is happening to you and know that there is still hope for you. Know that self-compassion isn't just about being nice to yourself, but it is a tool that helps you gain peace with your life's reality.

4. Work on Your Anger

Daughters of emotionally absent fathers often experience anger and frustration. Working on anger can help overcome grief and feelings of abandonment. The ability to control anger and remain stable in situations is beneficial to health and well-being.

Breathing exercises are an effective means of calming down and diverting one's attention. Physical and mental benefits of breathing exercises include the suppression of stress hormones. In times of anger, the brain sends signals to the body that it is in crisis, which is one reason why breathing exercises can be beneficial. Breathing exercises may be calming because slowing down breathing and focusing on one's breath signals to the brain that one is safe.

Breathing Exercises You Can Practice

The following are some of the breathing exercises you can do whenever you feel angry:

i. 4-7-8 Technique

The 4-7-8 technique by Dr. Andrew Weil is excellent for relieving anger and stress. This technique is one of the easiest to perform, and you can do it almost anywhere, at any time. Once you have mastered this breathing technique through daily, twice-daily practice, it will be a very useful tool that you will always carry.

How to do this?

Step 1: Make sure you are comfortable in your seat before starting the exercise. Shut your eyes and pay attention to how you're breathing. Remember to breathe deeply for a few minutes.

Step 2: Breathe in through the nose for four seconds; hold it for seven seconds; breathe out through the mouth for eight seconds.

Step 3: Repeat this process three times, then continue until you feel better or until the anger passes naturally.

ii. Diaphragmatic Breathing

Breathing through your diaphragm can help you relax; this type of breathing is useful in managing anger. When you breathe using your diaphragm, you will feel that your lungs are filling up completely with air. This helps release anger by shifting focus away from stressful thoughts or situations.

How to do this?

Step 1: Find a comfortable place where you can lie down. Wait until your body becomes quiet and still before starting the exercise. Relaxing music may be helpful as well.

Step 2: Raise your right arm straight above your head, keeping it straight all the time during the exercise. Place your right hand on the area between your shoulder and neck, just below your collarbone.

Step 3: Slowly inhale through your nose; in the middle of this breath, count to four seconds. At the same time, contract your hand between shoulder and neck, pulling in the air (this is called "the diaphragmatic breathing in the cycle"). Do this breathing cycle quickly, at least 10 times every day.

Step 4: Repeat this, breathing through both lungs once again. Do this exercise twice each day, in the morning and just before bed.

iii. Box Breathing

Box breathing, which is also called four-square breathing, is easy to learn and do. If you've ever noticed that you breathe in and out to the beat of a song, you've already done paced breathing.

How to do this?

Step 1: Exhale for four counts.

Step 2: Hold your breath for four counts.

Step 3: Inhale for four counts.

Step 4: Hold for four counts, then repeat the cycle.

Step 5: Take a few minutes to practice this several times until you get the hang of it. Once you are calm, resume your regular breathing exercises. If you notice an anger-provoking situation coming on, try box breathing during the stress's onset to prevent it from becoming a full-blown rage.

iv. Pursed-Lip Breathing

A simple way to make deep breaths slower and more deliberate is to breathe with your lips together. Pursed-lip breathing can offer you a sense of calm and relieve tension.

How to do this?

Step 1: Relax your neck and shoulders and find a good place to sit.

Step 2: Close your mouth and take a slow, two-second breath in through your nose.

Step 3: Exhale through your mouth for four seconds while making a kissing face with your lips.

Step 4: Inhale through your nose for four seconds.

Step 5: Rest for four seconds and repeat the cycle, emphasizing the exhale because it helps release built-up adrenaline. In this way, you can avoid anger in stressful situations by consciously deciding to relax.

Breathing techniques can be used as a coping tool anytime you are feeling angry—even right before an intense situation occurs. By practicing breathing techniques daily, you will be able to reduce and manage anger effectively.

5. Improve Social Skills

Social connection is important for mental and emotional health. Finding ways to connect with others, such as meeting friends or participating in interest groups, can help reduce isolation and loneliness and increase social connection. Cultivating social relationships is one way that you can improve your self-esteem.

Tips on Developing Healthy Relationships With Others

a. Listen and Support

Try to be supportive if you are the only person in the room with an opinion or viewpoint by listening to what others have to say and putting yourself in their shoes. Try to find something that you can agree on with them, and affirm them by saying, **"I see where you're coming from!"** or **"I think I see what you mean."** This demonstrates to others that you are interested in what they have to say and that they are not alone in the discussion. This will also make them like and appreciate you as a person because you are being supportive of them and their ideas.

Remember that you are having a conversation, not an argument. If you try to be persuasive in your conversation and make the other person feel like your point of view is superior to theirs, it will make them defensive, which makes it harder for them to understand what you are trying to say. If a person feels attacked by something you said, they will most likely not listen to what you had to say.

b. Be Respectful

When you find yourself in a group of people, try to be respectful towards the others in the group by discussing things that others agree upon and leaving controversial topics out of the conversation. Try not to argue with other people when you disagree with them because this will cause more conflict and leave other people feeling uncomfortable about what is being discussed. Not only will it make you look bad, but it will also give others a negative impression of you, as well. When you disagree, try to do so in a more respectful way by saying, **"I see where that point of view came from, but I believe it is different because** _____**."** If you disagree, don't make it seem as if you are trying to persuade people to see things your way; they will appreciate open-mindedness and the fact that you respect the way they feel about something.

Remember that you aren't the only person in a conversation. Consider what the other person might be feeling as they speak in an effort to put yourself in their position. Then, connect this to your own life in a manner that the other person can comprehend.

c. Give Credit Where Credit Is Due

When you find that you have something in common with someone or have learned something from them, be sure to give them credit for what they have said. This shows that you are appreciative of their efforts and respect their knowledge on a subject. It also makes them feel good about themselves because they will know that they were able to teach you something new and important about themselves or their field.

If you have been given something, be sure to show your appreciation by saying "Thanks!" or "Great!" If you need help with how to do this but are concerned about how your compliment will be received, try using a high voice, using big gestures, and often smiling. Having a big smile can seem fake if you aren't used to it, so it is important that you are not afraid of looking fake while being polite and showing your appreciation.

d. Try New Things

Introduce yourself to people by asking them questions about themselves or their interests. Make the conversation flow by asking questions or giving compliments.

For example, you can say, **"Hi, my name is _____; what are you here for?"** or **"I really like your shirt! Where did you buy it?"** People appreciate when you take an interest in them by asking questions about their lives. If you ask people about themselves first and make them feel appreciated, it will make them want to talk to you more, which, in turn, makes the conversation flow more smoothly.

If this isn't something you are used to doing when meeting someone new, try asking yourself questions such as **"What can I find out about this person?"** or **"How can I relate what they are saying to me?"** or **"How can I relate their interests to mine?"** When you are able to relate what they say to your own interests, it will make the conversation flow more smoothly because you are both interested in each other's lives. By asking questions and sharing interests with other people, you will become more confident and happy in your life.

e. Be Yourself!

It is important that you try to be yourself at all times. Remember that you only need your own approval to make yourself feel more confident about, so don't try to be someone else to be accepted. If you are trying to be someone that you aren't, people will notice very quickly, and it will be obvious to them that you aren't the person they thought you were. Don't feel like you need to dress a certain way just because you think it will make others more accepting of you. Dress in a manner that makes you feel at ease and be yourself!

Sometimes, it can be hard to feel confident about the "real" you, especially when you have put on a different self-image or identity for others. Try telling yourself something like, **"I am finally being real with myself"** or **"I don't have to pretend anymore. I am being who I really am."** Because it reminds you of your authenticity, this will help you feel better about yourself and your surroundings.

People will either like or dislike you for who you are; there is nothing you can do to change that. As long as you are sincere and authentic, you should not care what others think of you.

Overcoming your insecurity and low self-esteem is the most difficult thing you will ever have to do, but it will ultimately be worthwhile. First, you must realize how important it is for you to do this for yourself and how much it will affect your life. You can't expect yourself to make any improvements if you sit around and feel sorry for yourself because that is the surest way to keep feeling exactly how you are at this moment.

If you have determined that this is worthwhile for you, it's time to get started! The next question to ask yourself is, "What do I need to do first?" If you have never asked yourself this question, now is a good time to start.

CONCLUSION

Your father's presence in your life will provide you with opportunities to develop healthy relationships. He will help you learn how to share and express your feelings, making it possible for you to establish relationships based on trust and honesty.

The limitations of the father's presence, as well as his absence, will affect you in a number of ways. An emotionally absent father will leave a void in your life, creating an emptiness within you that can become overwhelming. You will experience a sense of insecurity and a lack of self-esteem, making it difficult for you to identify yourself. It will also make it difficult for you to develop healthy relationships with other people because your identity is tied up with your relationship with your father.

Nonetheless, it is essential to acknowledge that, like you, your father has personal circumstances that led to his emotional abandonment of you. Others may have physically, emotionally, or mentally abused him; he may have had no father figure growing up to learn how to be a good father himself. He might not have been given the opportunity to get an education and make a satisfactory living for his family. Alternatively, he may have a mental health condition such as anxiety or depression, making it difficult for him to provide you with the necessary nurturing and care. Whatever the case, if you can realize that your father is as much of a victim as you are, you will have a chance to be compassionate towards him and help him heal from his emotional trauma.

Despite this, there will be situations where you need to cut off your connection with him and begin your individual healing process, especially if the relationship between the two of you becomes dangerous and harmful. Knowing when and how to cut off your relationship with him can be difficult, but it can be done. It takes immense courage and strength to do so, but you will be rewarded with a healthy relationship in the future if you have the determination.

It is important to understand that your relationship with your father is not your fault. However, it does not mean that you are helpless. You can take steps towards healing and recovery from the emotional stress caused by being emotionally abandoned by your father. You can learn the skills necessary to move on with your life.

Always remember it is important to be kind to yourself, trust in the healing process, and recover from any past hurt because it can be very difficult. But it is not impossible. Having patience, courage, and determination will make this possible.